PARENTING IS A MINISTRY

by Pastor Craig F. Caster

PLEASE VISIT OUR WEBSITE
For FREE Marriage & Parenting
Resources
www.parentingministry.org

XULON
PRESS

www.xulonpress.com

Endorsements

"I have been using this material in my counseling with parents and in classes we teach at Shadow Mountain Community Church for over six years now. Craig's material is biblically sound, extremely practical, and right on target for our times. As a seminary trained pastor and marriage and family therapist, I whole heartedly and unreservedly recommend this material to parents and others who are looking for tools and God's direction on how to raise children into mature godly adults."

-Rev. Dr. Marcial Felan, Pastor of Family Ministries Shadow Mountain Community Church, El Cajon, California

"Somewhere along the line "discipleship" has vanished. Things that were once understood are now lost. The family unit is dangerously suffering. Why? Because of a lack of knowledge! That is… knowledge of God's design. The answer is to return to discipleship. Craig Caster is a man of God that I have observed for years. He truly has become a model of a "discipler," starting with the discipleship of his own family. I have also seen the fruit in my own church as well as other churches. Let's come back to discipleship, and here is a great book to start on parenting. I think you will find yourself becoming a disciple and then using these tools to disciple others, especially your own family."

-Pastor Bryan Newberry
Calvary Chapel San Diego, Chula Vista, California

"I have known Craig for many years. He has not only a vision to help families, but a call from God. Family Discipleship Ministries is an excellent, non-bureaucratic organization that is effective and faithful to its mission. We believe in this work of love and compassion for today's families and respectfully endorse it."

-Pastor Mike MacIntosh
Horizon Christian Fellowship, San Diego, California

"I have been personally involved with Family Discipleship Ministries since Pastor Craig started the ministry. I have watched as the Lord revealed to Craig the needs of the body of Christ then he prayerfully met them. Put your mind at ease, there is no worldly psychology in Craig's approach...rather Craig has addressed the needs of the family with the proven principles of the Word of God, pure and simple."

-Pastor Rob Hubbard
Calvary Chapel of Ramona, Ramona, California

Acknowledgments

As the author of this book, I see myself as merely an agent or messenger of what I have been shown or told.

I would like to acknowledge and give praise to the Lord Jesus Christ for answering my pleas as a young father who was struggling in how to raise my children correctly. He not only answered my prayers for wisdom as a parent through His Word and the Holy Spirit, He has also given me the privilege to minister these wonderful truths found in His Word to many others.

I want to thank my wife, Cha Cha, for her love and support of me and our children. My life has been made so rich because of her faithfulness to our Lord to love and serve me and our children.

To my parents, Terry and Barbara, who raised me and seven other brothers and sisters; they exemplified the importance of love and commitment to each other, and each of their children, along with being faithful in their walk with Jesus Christ – thank you.

My parents gave me my middle name, Francis, and my mom gave me this prayer by St. Francis of Assisi when I left the business world to answer the call to fulltime ministry.

Lord, make me an instrument of Your peace,
Where there is hatred, let me sow love,
Where there is injury, pardon,
Where there is doubt, faith,
Where there is despair, hope,
Where there is darkness, light, and
Where there is sadness, joy.
O Divine Master, grant that I may not so much seek
to be consoled as to console,
to be understood as to understand,
to be loved as to love.
For it is in pardoning that we are pardoned, and it
is in dying that we are born to eternal life.

Table of Contents

Foreword

"Growing up with the godly principles that are taught in this book has made me who I am today. Now that I am married and in full-time ministry, I can see the significant impact from the way I was raised and how it is affecting my life in every area. Working alongside my father in the ministry, I see first hand how these godly principles are blessing families throughout the world. I thank God for His teachings on parenting and my dad for surrendering and following through with what the Lord taught him."

Nick Caster (Authors oldest son)

"Now that I am a young adult, financially self sufficient and living alone thousands of miles away from my parents in a world full of sin, I know first hand the necessity of having character, personal responsibility, morals and values, and most importantly an abiding relationship with my Lord Jesus Christ. These tools are not learned by chance, and do not come with age. I, like everyone else, was born with the curse of sin and needed to be taught how to deny myself and take up the duty of being a warrior for

Christ. I have my parents to thank for that. I don't thank them for being wise, or following a magical formula that guarantees a mature adult. I thank them for obeying the voice of God and for being a living example of what it means to be a man, a woman, a husband, a wife, a father, a mother, and a child of God. I believe with all of my being that the contents found in this book come directly from God's Word, and I will use it to raise my own children when the time comes. Craig Caster didn't unravel the secrets of parenting, he simply read God's Word, listened to His voice, and put His teachings in a book for all to understand. Craig is a vessel, and I couldn't be more proud to call him dad."

Justin Caster (Authors youngest son)

Introduction

"Many current authors offer practical advice to encourage parents in the latest trends for family life. However, few appear to go deep to the foundation and source of authentic parenting as rooted in the Biblical principles as seen through God's example as Parent. I believe Craig Caster truly captures the heart of our Heavenly Father as He would model a discipleship paradigm; where parents have the divine privilege of equipping their children to grow in the image of Jesus Christ through intentional training. Not only does Craig assist parents to practically grasp God's eternal parenting model, he lives it out with his own family as a testimony of God's eternal plan. It is no small wonder that this theme is a priority in God's work in the world as He concludes the entire Old Testament with the challenge, 'And he will turn the hearts of the fathers to the children, and the hearts of the children to their fathers, lest I come and strike the earth with a curse.' (Malachi 4:6 NKJV)"

Mickey Stonier Ph.D.
Adjunct Professor at Azusa Pacific University,
Graduate School of Theology and Talbot Seminary

Preface

All parents experience struggles and difficulties in raising their children. Some may struggle with how to work together as a team (if married); others with how to adapt to their children's unique personalities and interests, but more often than not, most parents have difficulty in the area of disciplining their children correctly. The truth is most parents today feel they did not have a good role model from their parents so they feel ill-equipped to parent.

God, as the Creator of the institution we call family, has given us clear instructions in His Word on how it is to be done. It is Satan's main objective to attack and destroy the families to make weak one's testimony, the church, society, and our nation. God, knowing this, gave us both His Word to guide us and His Holy Spirit to strengthen us to overcome and have victory over Satan's attacks.

Sadly, most Christians do not believe the Bible has anything relevant to say about raising children in today's world, hence, they are not looking to God and instead are relying on personal experiences or worldly advice. Our God, who is All-Knowing and loving, knew Satan's plans so He provided us with His Word and Holy Spirit to help all generations of people, but if we do not look to Him for guidance and strength to tend to our families then what should we expect to happen?

I know this book will bless you and bring clarity to God's will for raising children as a traditional family, blended family, single parent family, or grandparents raising grandchildren. God loves us and our children too much to leave us ignorant to these wonderful life changing parenting principles. May God bless you and your family as you allow Him to transform you into the parent He knows you can be.

Prologue

His Precious Gifts

I have three children. I love them all and want the best for them, but I have fallen so short in comparison to God's love toward me. There were times that I did not always have the best thoughts toward my children when they were growing up. In my ignorance I thought, "Oh my gosh! God, I think you made a mistake. This one is defective." I have come to understand that God did not make a mistake and none of them are defective. In His perfect wisdom, He gave me the gifts He knew that I needed.

Who are the gifts God has given to you? We learn in Psalm 127 that our children are a gift from God. So my question is not what are the gifts, but who are the gifts that God has given to you? What have you done with the gifts that He has given to you? How have you valued them? How do you think God would perceive the way you have handled, or mishandled, the gifts that He has given to you?

In the past I thought that God was always very disappointed with me. Every time I would consider what God must be thinking about me, I perceived that He was thinking, "Craig, you ding-dong. When are you gonna get it together? Ok, that's it. That's the last time Craig." I had a terrible idea of how God viewed me after the things I had done in my life. I thought He was downright upset and angry with me all the time. But, I learned that this thinking was a lie from Satan.

If you went to the beach and scooped two handfuls of sand, the grains of sand in your two hands would outnumber all the seconds you would live for the rest of your natural life. God says that all His thoughts toward us are good and they out number all the grains of sand in the whole earth (Psalm 139:17-18). With all of these good thoughts, when can our Creator have a bad thought about us?

He predestined all of our days, including the "bad days" and the difficult trials that will come and touch our lives. God knows as imperfect parents that we may have made some mistakes. He knew before He created us that we would make these mistakes. But God uses our mistakes through the trials and difficulties in our lives to reveal Himself to us and to call us into a closer relationship with Him. Within His providential permission, He allows you and I to do some foolish things, but there are consequences. We see the consequences in many families today, non-Christians and Christians alike, because parents have been leaning on their own understanding in how they are to raise their children, creating such pain and confusion resulting in a lack of peace, joy and fruit of the Spirit in the lives of the parents and the kids.

Praise God He does not leave us or forsake us when we do such foolish things with His precious gifts (Hebrews 13:5). It is so important to remember that God will never leave or forsake (abandon) His children (us). But let us receive the discipline of our Lord so that we can share in His peace and righteousness in our homes. Remember, God knew every single one of us before time itself including the good, the bad, and the ugly (Psalm 139:1-18) and He still chose us to be His children. Praise God for that!

In Luke chapter 15, Jesus speaks to a mixed group of believers and non-believers, commoners and elitists, about His relationship with His children. He was saying to them (and to us), "Listen to me and I will teach you how My Father in Heaven looks upon His children." It is glorious when we really come to know and understand this.

In Luke 15:4-7, Jesus begins speaking the parable of the lost sheep and how God lovingly pursues us when we go astray. In Luke 15:8-10 Jesus tells us the parable of the lost coin demonstrating the value that God places upon each one of us, and how precious and unique each of us are to Him. In the parable commonly known as "The Prodigal Son" in Luke 15:11-24, Jesus teaches us about the gifts that God has given to His children. God has given every one of us gifts that He says are for us. We are to perceive our spouse and our children as very special gifts from God.

A prodigal son is someone who took what his father has given to him and then misused and abused it according to his own way. Even when we foolishly abuse His gifts to us, just like the prodigal son had abused his gifts, God is not thinking, "Oh you stupid idiot." In His foreknowledge, He already knew we would do the things we have done. His love, His mercy and His ways are so beyond our understanding. This is why Jesus takes the time to say, "Listen to me. I want you to know how God thinks about you. Don't rely upon your own understanding. I want you to know My Father. I want you to know His thoughts towards you."

In Luke 15:11-13 Jesus tells us that, "A certain man had two sons and the younger of them said to his father, 'Father, give me the portion of goods that fall to me.' So he divided to them his livelihood. And not many days after, the younger son gathered all together and journeyed to a far country and there wasted his possession with prodigal living." Notice it was the son speaking to his father asking for his portion of goods and then going his own way. As His sons and daughters, this message is directed to us.

When the prodigal son says, "give me the portion of goods that fall to me", he is telling his father, "give me all that is coming to me now." He is not asking for more, just what's coming to him. In a sense this is us saying to our heavenly Father, "I want it all God. Give me those blessings you promised me." Do you want all of God's gifts He has for you? It's not wrong to say, "God, give me all that You have for me." In fact, He wants us to say, "I want it all, God. Since You have gifts for me. I want them all." The sad reality is that most of us treat the gifts He has given to us recklessly. When we don't look upon His gifts as blessings, we treat them incorrectly.

How many of us have treated our spouse or our children, God's gifts, inappropriately? How many of us do not know what to do with the gifts He has given to us? By the time my oldest son was three I wanted to wrap that gift up and send him back. Even at such a young age, he could do things to make me angrier than any human being on earth. He wasn't eighteen pounds yet and at that point I was two hundred pounds. I was praying, "God where can I go and trade this one in? I think you made a mistake! This one is broken."

Praise God much has changed since then. One of the greatest things that has changed in me is my attitude toward my strong-willed child. God gave to me the understanding that my son is His gift to my wife and to me. My anger problem was not my son's fault or responsibility. The problem was with me. God used this strong-willed child to reveal my selfish foolish heart, and to bring me to my knees. As I began to pray and fast and say, "God, help me," He began to transform me.

That's the purpose of the trials in raising our children. God brings us to the point where we say, "Lord, I need help. I don't know what I'm doing here. You say that my son (daughter) is a gift, but he (she) doesn't seem like a gift." That's when God says, "He (She) is a very special gift, and, if you come to Me, I'll show you how to treat him (her). I'll show you how to take care of him (her)." God had to do some real surgery to transform my heart and mind, and teach me how to properly value and treat His precious gift.

We read in verse twelve and thirteen where the son said to his father, "give me all that is coming to me." What he was saying in essence was, "OK, I'm ready father. I'm ready to take care of all the things that I own. I do not need your help or support to take care of them anymore. I can do it on my own." Then he went out on his own and wasted his possessions with prodigal (reckless, wasteful, selfish) living. This son did not use or treat the gifts his father had given to him properly, but instead he abused them and wasted them according to his own desires. He took the gifts that were coming to him and foolishly said, "You know what? I am not going to follow your way, dad. I don't want your help anyway. I don't need your support. I am going to take these gifts and use them the way I want to."

This is the first part of the message of the prodigal son. When somebody receives gifts from God and then treats or uses those gifts in a different way than God intended, they are living as the prodigal son; recklessly, wastefully, selfishly and foolishly. Why are so many within the body of Christ living as prodigals? Because they have been blinded to this condition by leaning upon their own understanding, by trusting in the false teachings of the world and the lack of effective discipling within the church. Some of us have neglected the gifts He has given to us. Others of us are ignorant to what God wants us to do with His gifts. And some of us are simply in rebellion.

Have you ever looked upon your spouse and your children as gifts from God? As you probably already know the divorce rate is staggering. But did you know that approximately one-half of all divorces claim to believe in Jesus as their Lord and Savior, and go to church? Divorce is one of the most painful and confusing things that can happen in the life of a child. How many of us are not currently treating our spouse as God desires? If we do not daily look to Jesus for wisdom, strength and power, then we will lean upon our own strength and foolishness as the prodigal son did. Instead of properly caring for our spouse and children, as God desires, we treat them as we desire foolishly and selfishly. Many are on the path to becoming a part of the above mentioned statistics and/or they will continue to live in a strained unfulfilling relationship with their spouse and children if the church does not do a better job of discipling them in these areas.

Many relationships between husband and wife become strained because they are not unified in their methods for raising their children. The relationship between the parents and the children is strained because the parents do not know how to love and train their children the way God desires. Instead there is yelling, disrespecting one another, arguing, manipulation and inconsistency. When I finally realized this condition in my own life and I said, "Lord, please help me." In His mercy He didn't turn me away.

What does this son eventually do in the midst of his circumstances? In verse 17 we read, "...but when he came to himself, he said, 'how many of my father's hired servants have bread enough to spare, and I perish with hunger'?" There are some very important messages in this verse. The son came to his senses (yielded to the conviction of the Holy Spirit) and thought to himself, "Of course I should go to my dad. He's the one who had the gifts. He's the one who gave them to me. He knows how to take care of them. I need to go back to him." This he did because he had come to the end of himself.

There are many people on plan number nine hundred and ninety nine that refuse to admit that they are at the end of themselves. Their marriage lacks true companionship, love and unity. Their relationship with their children is strained and out of order. Instead of coming to the Lord they devise an inferior plan. They decide either on their own or with "help" from a friend, or read some book giving worldly counsel and suddenly they conclude to embark on their "new" surefire plan without asking the One who gave their gifts to them. The prodigal son went to the world and the world had nothing for him. When will we also realize the world cannot help us? There is only One who can! The prodigal son had to come to the end of himself before he would return to his father. What kind of crisis will it take before we will come to the end of ourselves and go to our Father and ask Him for his help.

Why, for so many, does it take a huge crisis before we go to our Savior and say, "Lord, help me"? God wants us to come to Him, but Satan has done a masterful job in the body of Christ to get us to believe that the Word of God is not applicable to these areas of our lives. Satan has convinced many that God is weak, unconcerned, unable or unwilling to help us. Now we would never say such a thing with our lips, but look at the condition of the body of Christ. We're saying it in our daily lives.

It's by God's grace alone that we are able to take care of His gifts. Did you know that in every area of your life where you are not experiencing the power, the peace and the understanding of God, it is because you have not truly brought it to God? What will it take for you to really begin to look to Him for the wisdom, the strength and the understanding of how to take care of your spouse and children? Proverbs 3:5-6 tells us to, "Trust in the Lord with all your heart and lean not on your own understanding. But in <u>all</u> your ways acknowledge Him and He shall direct your path." Do you know what the word all means? Nothing is excluded. Everything is included. Are you ready to look to Him and say, "God, please help me" and then be willing to follow His instructions?

This story continues so wonderfully in verses 18 – 19, "I will rise and go to my father and I will say to him, Father, I have sinned against heaven and before you and I am no longer worthy to be called your son. Make me like one of your hired servants." This is important to understand. When some of us come to Christ, we try to make a deal with Him. You know what, God does not negotiate. "Ok God, I'll love my husband, but if he does not do this or that…forget it!" "Lord, if you don't give me what I want, then you know what? I don't have time for You." Or we say to God through our daily lives, "I'll go to church on Sunday, but I am to busy to spend time with you each day." "When my son or my daughter quits acting this way, then I will quit screaming and yelling at them. If they start obeying everything I say, then I will quit acting this way.

There is never justification for our sinful behavior. We cannot rightfully say to any other person, "You made me sin." Why do you think God gives to us such a complete definition of what love is and what love is not in His Word? When parents hear how this love applies to raising children, many times the parents begin weeping because often times there are four or five things that God says love is not that they do every single day to their spouse and/or to their children. You know what the opposite of love is? Hate. God calls it sin. You can't practice sin and expect God's grace and blessings and intercession because He is righteous.

As we look to verses 20 – 24, what does the prodigal son's father do? "…when he was still a great way off, his father saw him and had compassion and ran to him, fell on his neck and kissed him. And the son said to his father, "I have sinned against heaven and in your sight and I am no longer worthy to be called your son." But the father said to his servants, "Bring out the best robe and put it on him. And put a ring on his finger, and sandals on his feet. And bring the fatted calf here and kill it and let us eat and be merry, for my son was dead and is alive again. He was lost and he is found, and they began to be merry."

He was not in the house all upset thinking, "My jerk son is ruining my name out there and making me look like a dirt bag. Taking my gifts and throwing them away and wasting them. You know what, I hope he never comes back." He was not in his house complaining and whining and fretting over the foolishness of his son. Instead the father was waiting for his prodigal son to come home to him. This is a picture of your heavenly Father. He is waiting and hoping that you will come to Him everyday to receive wisdom and grace to take care of the spouse and children He gave to you. He knows your mistakes. Remember that He knows you better than you know yourself. He chose you and gave you these gifts.

He is not going to come to you and take them back. We can abuse them so much that we can lose them – yes. In His sovereignty He allows us the freedom to choose. But your God is waiting with His arms stretched out for you to come to Him so He can wrap His arms around you and kiss you and bless you. He never intended us to do anything relying on our own wisdom or our own strength. He is waiting and hoping that you will come to Him. He is not waiting for you to quit being angry on your own. He knows you cannot change on your own. He wants you to come to Him and receive the blessings with which He so lovingly desires to bless you.

God knows our sin and our weaknesses better than we know ourselves. He knows that we have been trying to do things in our own way. He knows that we have turned to worldly sinful things to deal with the pain that comes from not looking to Him first to care for His gifts the way that He desires. But His love is awesome. His grace and His mercy are also wonderful gifts. He wants us to come to Him and He will meet you right where you are now and begin to instill in you His wisdom, strength and power to fulfill His will in how to treat your gifts the way He desires.

My hope is that when you have completed this book you will see your children through His eyes as His gifts to you. That you will be better prepared to love and care for them, as He desires. I pray that you will be willing to cast aside all of your traditional views about parenting and be willing to learn through His Word by the Holy Spirit what He would have you do with His gifts. I know by God fulfilling His promises in my family that no matter what is in your past or how you have previously treated His gifts, that He is eagerly waiting with great anticipation for you to embrace Him and His ways to be the parent He has called you to be. His Word reveals that these are His children He has given to you and His Word is His instruction manual. Follow Him and He will bless you.

Are you really ready to follow Him now? "Take My yoke upon you and learn from Me, for I am gentle and humble in heart, and YOU WILL FIND REST FOR YOUR SOULS. For My yoke is easy and My burden is light." (Matthew 11:29 – 30)

Prayer

Father, I want to thank You for Your grace and Your mercy for me. Thank You for Your Word. Thank You that You are so patient. Thank You that You are waiting patiently with your arms stretched out for me to come to You everyday. I believe that You want to bless me. I believe that You want to give me wisdom. I believe that You want to empower me, Lord, with Your grace to love and train my children. Thank You that I can come into Your presence anytime and anyplace. I ask You to help me to learn to hear Your voice, to know Your will for caring for the children You have put into my care. Help me Lord to be willing to invest the time to learn what Your Word has to say. I pray that Your Holy Spirit will guide me and give to me the understanding of Your Word. Lord I repent of my ways and I am willing to denounce all other worldly wisdom. I ask for forgiveness for turning to these things. I pray that you would be glorified. I ask these things in Jesus' name. Amen.

CHAPTER ONE

Where Do We Turn?

In the Beginning Was Frustration

When I first began using a computer, I discovered something profound: no matter how valuable the tool, if you do not understand how to use it properly, it can be a source of great frustration. Today, I am relatively proficient on the computer, but when I first started, I encountered much difficulty. The learning curve was a terrible thing for me! Several times I would work an hour or more on a message, and then it would "disappear" before I had a chance to save it. Despite my valiant efforts—pushing buttons, phoning less technologically-challenged friends—my message was gone. I was so frustrated; I was tempted to throw the darn computer across the room! But once I understood how my computer worked, once I understood which buttons performed which tasks, it actually became an awesome tool!

Parenting is much the same. Within a few months of bringing your beautiful baby home from the hospital, you find yourself filled with anxiety. Why is he crying? What does he want? So you scramble around, devise a plan, and run with it. Then right when you think you have it down, fifteen to eighteen months comes around, when he really starts moving—even standing up and running—causing more anxiety, more frustration, and you are forced to adapt your methods to this new state of affairs. Just when you think you have mastered the childhood stage, adolescence comes, and it starts all over.

And somewhere in there, your second, third, maybe fourth child comes along. If you have multiple children, you have already discovered that God has a sense of humor—none of your kids are exactly the same, so the techniques you learned with the first one often have a completely different effect on the succeeding children.

However, despite the frustration, parenting is incredibly rewarding. Whether you have one child or several, you already realize that as a parent you have taken on an enormous responsibility, fraught with potential difficulties, but also filled with much joy and delight. Just watching your children grow, seeing the dynamics as they interact, and noticing the change in their personalities is so interesting! And the best news of all: parenting is fun, when you learn to embrace the challenge with biblical understanding to God's will in raising them. Thankfully, effective parenting does not have to be a mystery. God *wants* us to understand our role and purpose as parents, what He wants us to accomplish, where our responsibility starts and stops; in other words, which buttons perform which tasks.

Our Past Experiences May Not Be Enough

When you look back into your adolescence, do you believe that your parents really knew what they were doing? Most of us, looking back, are fairly certain that our parents used a "hit-and-miss" kind of philosophy; they were not really sure what they were doing.

Now, in view of your current method ... who taught you how to be a parent? Typically, as Christians, we take the good things we think our parents did, throw out the bad, and make up the rest, based upon our personalities and past experiences. Since it is rare that both the husband and the wife had exactly the same type of upbringing, the most common method is for you each to reflect upon your own childhoods, then come together and try to work out a system based upon those experiences and each of your personalities. But by the time your child is three, you realize that he or she is not like you at all, either one of you! And you begin to realize that the parenting you are doing may not be affecting this particular child in the way you intended.

This brings us to the first key to effective parenting: *it is vitally important for us to look to God's Word, not our past experiences*. Many times I have heard parents say, "Well, I always thought as long as I was doing the job better than my parents, my kids would turn out at least as good as me. At least I am not screaming and beating them. I had it much worse than them." That is a very common philosophy. Yet the only philosophy that you and I should use, the only road map, is God's Word; He wants us to know how we are supposed to accomplish this very difficult task and has given us complete access to that information.

The Original Blueprint

In order to follow God's plan for parenting, we must first look to the original blueprint. It was God, not man, who created the institution of family, and it was the first, therefore most important, institution He created.

> And the LORD God said, "It is not good that man should be alone; I will make him a helper comparable to him." And the LORD God caused a deep sleep to fall on Adam, and he slept; and He took one of his ribs, and closed up the flesh in its place. Then the rib which the LORD God had taken from man He made into a woman, and He brought her to the man. Therefore a man shall leave his father and mother and be joined to his wife, and they shall become one flesh. And Then God blessed them, and God said to them, "Be fruitful and multiply; fill the earth and subdue it; have dominion over the fish of the sea, over the birds of the air, and over every living thing that moves on the earth."
>
> —Genesis 2:18, 21-22, 24; 1:28

The reason marriage in the United States is, for the most part, made up of one wife and one husband (although that is rapidly changing) is because of the Christian influence in our country. In other parts of the world, they still practice man's way—have many wives, treat them as possessions, have someone else raise the kids. That system, man's idea of family, is still in operation in some countries today.

But of the institution of family that God created, He said, "A husband and wife will come together and have children" (paraphrase, Gen. 1:28). It is this pattern, God's design, God's plan for families, which we must view as our model to successful parenting.

The majority of couples already have discovered that it is hard enough as a husband and wife to come together; then you add two or three children and their personalities, and everything becomes much more complicated. Our personal desire for fulfillment, our own selfish expectations get in the way all the time. We put those desires and expectations upon our kids, and when they do not meet them, we get angry; we revert to our flesh.

It would be a dirty trick for God to put us in a situation like that, as important and complex as it is to raise children, and not give us some clear guidelines in how to accomplish it successfully. God, of course, does not play dirty tricks. Scripture tells us, *"The Lord is righteous in all His ways, gracious in all His works"* (Ps. 145:17).

A survey taken in 1998 showed that less than 11 percent of Christians believe that the Bible has anything relevant or significant to say about raising kids[1]. Less than 11 percent! That is tragic! Sadly, Satan has done a masterful job of deceiving us. In truth, God loves our children far more than we ever will, and He wants so much for you and me to know how to parent correctly. He wants our actions to glorify His love toward His children.

It is imperative we understand that *God's Word is complete and contains all we need to be successful.* His desire is for us to know what He wants us to do.

In Genesis 18:19, God said to Abraham:

For I have known him, in order that he may command his children and his household after him, that they keep the way of the LORD, to do righteousness and justice, that the LORD may bring to Abraham what He has spoken to him.

Just as Abraham was told to "command his children," we also must teach our children *with intention*, be *intentional* about our ways, be *intentional* about following what God says regarding the raising up of our children. Once we begin to perceive our job as that of ministers over our children, and to understand that it is our relationship to Christ that gives us the wisdom, strength, and power to accomplish this very difficult task of raising children, we can begin to unlock the secret to successful parenting.

---

[1] Churches Have Opportunity to Help Parents, Barna Group, January 15, 1998

CHAPTER TWO

God's Purposes for Parenting

A Minister! Who Me?

When we hear the word "minister," we often have certain ideas attached to the word: "that's a pastor or someone who works in the church." In reality, what is a minister? The word *minister* in the *Webster Dictionary* means "one who acts under the order of another, or who is employed by another to execute his purpose." As a verb, *to minister* means "to adjust, regulate, or set in order[1]."

What does this mean to us? As Christians, we are under Jesus Christ—God—and He is the One from whom we receive our instructions. And God has given us His children to parent, so that we might execute His purposes over them. So you and I are ministers over our children, under God. It is so important that we perceive our task in that mindset, because it completely changes our approach when it comes to the raising up of our kids.

As a minister of our Lord Jesus Christ, our disposition must be to fulfill His will and purpose in all things through our lives. Having total dependence upon Him is essential. We are not to serve our children's wills and wishes, but to serve the *Lord* and fulfill *His* will and desires for our children.

Certainly Jesus Christ is the best example of a minister. Matthew 20:28 says of Jesus, *"Even as the Son of man came not to be **ministered** unto, but to **minister**, and to give His life a ransom for many"* (KJV, emphasis added).

The New King James Version of the same passage tells us, *"Just as the Son of Man did not come to be **served**, but to **serve**, and to give His life a ransom for many."*

Clearly, a minister is also a servant. When we see our job or responsibility of "parent" being that of a servant, a minister over our children, versus the worldly view of parenting, it changes our entire outlook.

His Goals

As a minister, we must know God's purpose; what does He want us to do and accomplish? Understanding His purposes helps us recognize our genuine need for God's daily wisdom and strength.

The word "purpose" means an intended or desired result or goal[2]. If I interviewed two hundred parents and asked them what they believe God's purpose is for them as ministers, as parents, I would likely get two hundred different answers. Not even many husbands and wives would be unified regarding their purpose. To a certain extent, that is a problem, because as we have seen, husbands and wives are supposed to be working together. When those who are united in marriage have two different goals and purposes, they end up going in two different directions. And that is not God's plan!

Sadly, for some reason over the last fifty years or so, the body of Christ has not given preference to training or discipling people in parenting. Most churches have never had a parenting class! Our teenagers will get fifty hours or more of training to get a driver's license[3], yet how many hours of training do most parents go through on raising their kids? None. Which is more important, driving a car or raising kids? Obviously, raising children, by far! And due to that lack of training, many parents, even Christian parents, are the most negative influence on their children, more even than that of the world.

I counsel between twenty and thirty Christian families per month. I have found that, in most cases, it is not the music, the drugs, or the influence of the schools that is affecting the kids. It is what is going on inside the four walls of their homes. Of course it is not because these couples got married and said, "We want to mess up our kids." It is because they are just doing it their own way.

What happens, then, when a husband and wife disagree and are not clear in their God-given purposes? There are problems, there is tension, there is strife, there is division. There is a strain on the marriage, and that is a common problem today in the body of Christ.

It is clear, then, that the basis of our strong foundation must be an understanding of the purposes and plans that God has for us and through us. This will be the topic of the following section. Therefore, since God has purposes *for* us, and He also has purposes *through* us, when we understand what God is trying to do through us, and also what He is trying to do inside us, it helps us to embrace His work, and to see why it is so vital that we have a right relationship with Christ. Let us examine God's purposes for parents.

First Purpose: Our Transformation

"But whoever keeps His word, truly the love of God is perfected in him. By this we know that we are in Him" (1 John 2:5). The word *perfected* means "to make complete[4]" . . . in other words, a process. Being transformed into Christ's image is a process. God uses the dynamics of our household, the personalities of our children, and the stages that they are going through to transform us.

We like to tell ourselves, when we act in anger or in the flesh, "My kids made me act this way." Go ahead and find that in the Word! God says, "Nope, that was already in you. I am using this kid to bring it out of you, yet you keep looking at him as if he's making you act this way!" It is vitally important that you and I understand as ministers that God is using the dynamics of our families to purge us and transform us into the likeness of Christ.

In my own life, God particularly used my oldest son, Nicholas. At the time, because of my whole concept of discipline and rules, defiance and rebellion, I was so disturbed by Nicholas' behavior that I took everything he did the wrong way. By the time he was three years old, God used him to reveal the greatest anger within me.

When Nicholas was six years old, God finally got my attention. He said, "Craig, that's Me. That's not Nick. I'm just using him to bring about this transformation in you." I have discovered, over the years, that God has used my son Nicholas, my little mule, as one of the most powerful tools to transform me into Christ's image. Just like He's doing that with the mule that He has blessed you with!

I love the way Isaiah 29:16 is translated in the New Living Translation:

> *How foolish can you be? He is the Potter, and He is certainly greater than you, the clay! Should the created thing say of the one who made it, "He didn't make me"? Does a jar ever say, "The potter who made me is stupid"?*

Ouch! So many times in a heated moment, when God is trying to bring about transformation, we tell Him through our actions, "Take Your fingers off of me! Get Your hands off me, Lord! I don't want to be shaped, I don't want to be transformed. I'll be darned if I'm going to look at this little mule right now, whose head I want to take off, and believe that is You!" We must remember, however, that it *is* Christ who brings about or permits these circumstances, and that He uses them to reveal things in us that are ugly and do not glorify Him.

Knowing this, next time one of those heated moments comes, we can stop for a second and think, "Oh! Wait a minute, God, that's You. I'll be darned if I tell you to get Your hands off of me again. I'm not going to do that, Lord!"

It is very difficult for us as parents to give, love, and serve our kids when we feel like we are not getting anything back from them. It seems like we give, give, give, and they just take, take, take. But look at Jesus—how many times did someone walk up to Jesus and say, "Thanks Jesus! I'm so glad You're here"? Look at Moses. No one ever said, "Hey, Moses, thanks." Ministry is oftentimes a thankless job.

We need to see and understand that God has a purpose in the trials that He brings through our kids. It is almost impossible to embrace these trials and this transformation that is taking place if our eyes are not upon Christ. When our eyes are not upon Christ and these circumstances come about, we react from our flesh. So often parents justify this sinful attitude and response to their kids and tell themselves, "They made me act this way." But God says, "No, that's not the way it works."

Second Purpose: God's Glorification

"For you were bought at a price; therefore glorify God in your body and in your spirit, which are God's" (1 Cor. 6:20).

"Let your light so shine before men, that they may see your good works and glorify your Father in Heaven" (Matt. 5:16).

The word *glorify* means "to reflect[5]." You and I, as ministers, as Christians, must consider this purpose. We need to be glorifying God, acting as His reflection, to our children. If I gave your kids a good description of what Jesus looked and acted like, would they say that you glorify Him all the time in your home? As ministers, as Christians, we must be concerned about glorifying God to those whom we are ministering over.

A paraphrase of the story of Moses in Numbers 20:8-13 is a great example of this. The story reveals that Moses had to walk through the desert with two or three million people for forty years. We know how many heartaches and headaches, how much bickering and whining he had to put up with. Those people were whiners, despite the fact that they had God right in front of them as a cloud by day and a pillar of fire by night! He fed them out of the thin air, had bread fall from Heaven, and still they whined and complained.

Why do we put expectations upon our kids that God did not put upon the people Moses ministered over? At the end of the passage, the children of Israel were once again complaining—they needed water. "Our sheep are going to die; Moses, do something!" So Moses got alone with God, and God said, "I know they're thirsty. Go speak to the rock." But what did Moses do? He started walking over to the rock he was supposed to speak to, and he forgot who he was ministering for and who he was ministering over. He put his own selfish expectations upon those people, "These whining, selfish people! Despite all that God does, they're complaining and whining *again*!" By the time he got to that rock, he was upset! So instead of just saying, "Water, come forth," he grabbed his stick and struck it. And water came out.

But when Moses got alone with the Lord, the Lord said, "Moses, why did you strike that rock? I'm not mad at them. Now they think I'm mad at them. You misrepresented me, Moses. I told you to go and *speak* to the rock, that's all. Why did you go and strike it? Why did you put your selfish expectations upon these people and allow that to dictate what I've called you to do?"

How often do we misrepresent God in our house? Oftentimes Christian parents are more concerned about how strangers see them outside their four walls than they are about what their children see inside their four walls. That is hypocrisy, and that is one of the main reasons so many teenagers are walking away from the Lord. They watch us; they know everything about us. They know how easily we act out in the flesh. And when they see us at home doing things that they never see us do outside the four walls of our house, what is the message? We must be concerned with glorifying God within our homes! Even those of you who are in ministry must remember that the first ministry you have is your family.

Third Purpose: Love Them

Our third purpose is to love our children: "*Behold, children are a heritage from the LORD, the fruit of the womb is a reward*" (Ps. 127:3). The value we should place upon our children and the way we should treat them is determined by God's Word, not their personalities, stages of life, or their failures. God has determined the value of our children, and He dictates how we must treat them.

Fourth Purpose: To Train Them

Finally, our fourth and most obvious purpose is to train our children. "*And you, fathers, do not provoke your children to wrath, but bring them up in the training and admonition of the Lord*" (Eph. 6:4).

"Bring them up" is to raise our children to maturity, to educate them. Purposes three and four will also be addressed more fully in later chapters of this book.

No Exceptions

Please understand, none of these principles change if you are a single parent or part of a blended family. God did not give exclusions. There have been blended families and single-parent families for over four thousand years. God's Word applies to the single parent and the blended family, as equally as to the traditional two-parent family.

But I want to say this to the single parents, mothers and fathers; one of the most difficult things in the world is to raise kids alone. My twin sister has three children. I was there when their father left and saw the pain those kids went through. Divorce is an ugly thing, a difficult thing. It has been a hard road for my sister, but God has met her every step of the way. I also have counseled many single parents over the last twelve years.

Scripture promises: "*A father of the fatherless, a defender of widows, is God in His holy habitation*" (Ps. 68:5). God mentions the fatherless forty-one times in the Scriptures, and He mentions the widow seventy-four times. This shows us God's heart is upon the single-parent family!

We often think the word *widow* means a wife who has lost her husband to death, but in Christ's day, it meant much more than that. The Greek word *chera,* translated to "widow," is derived from the word *casma,* meaning the deficiency or vacancy of somebody. A widow was a woman who was simply deficient of a husband.

We often think that single parenting is a new thing. It is not. In Christ's day, all it took to put away a wife was a certificate, and a priest to sign it. It was a big problem. God knows and He cares. James 1:27 says, "*Pure and undefiled religion before God and the Father is this: to visit orphans and widows in their trouble, and to keep oneself unspotted from the world.*"

Again, if you are a single parent or in a blended family, all of the instructions and principles contained in this book apply to you. Thankfully, God's Word promises that He will help you and give you the strength to apply each one of these principles to your own situation.

"Come to Me, all you who labor and are heavy laden, and I will give you rest" (Matt. 11:28).

". . . The helpless commits himself to You; You are the helper of the fatherless" (Ps. 10:14).

I want to encourage you, single parents and blended families; you can do it in the power of Christ!

[1] Webster's New International Dictionary of the English Language; Second Edition Unabridged; G & C Merriam Company, Publishers, Springfield, MA 1944

[2] Webster's II New Riverside Dictionary Revised Edition, Office Edition, Houghton Mifflin Company, 1996

[3] http://www.dmv.org/ca-california/drivers-training.php

[4] Webster's New International Dictionary of the English Language; Second Edition Unabridged; G & C Merriam Company, Publishers, Springfield, MA 1944

[5] The Complete Word Study Dictionary, New Testament, 1392 Zodhiates, 1992 by AMG International, Inc. Revised Edition 1993

CHAPTER THREE

Building the Foundation

Prior to being in the ministry, I was a developer. I built industrial parks, shopping centers, and mini storages. Many years ago, we bought a piece of property in Temecula, California. We decided to put an office building on this particular piece of land. So we did a preliminary cost analysis to find out what we could afford, what would be the best rent, so on and so forth. We ran some numbers on it, it looked good, so we went ahead with the deal.

But when the architect finished with the plans, the foundation was much larger than previous similar developments we had built; the extra cost nearly blew the whole project. The footings were seven foot in diameter and used four times the amount of steel we had calculated for the foundation. I said to the architect, "What is this? We ran some preliminary numbers, we know what these buildings take . . . what happened?"

He replied, "Basically, Craig, there's a thing called 'liquefaction' about thirty feet under the crust of Temecula. Your property is on a big fault line, a huge level of mud. Because of that, you have two ways you can go: you can drive some huge pylons down and create an elaborate system, or you can build this massive foundation underneath the building."

Imagine what would have happened, however, if I took those plans and said, "I know you're an architect and you're supposed to know what you're doing, but I'm going to change it. I've built well over three million square feet by this time; I know what I'm doing. I'm going to build it the way I think is right."

So if I took those plans and I shrunk the foundation to how I thought it should be, what would happen after I built that building? No matter how beautiful it turned out, there would be a problem. It probably would not fall down right away, but we all know what happens in California: earthquakes. Even without an earthquake, we would have some storms, some strong winds, and those probably would not make the whole thing fall, but what would begin to happen is what we call "stress cracks." The slab would begin to break and separate, there would soon be cracks in the windows, and the door jambs would get to the point where they were tweaked and the doors would not close, then the staircase would begin cracking, and the elevator shaft would not line up. Eventually, they would condemn the building because of the storms and the resulting damage.

Obviously it would be foolish for me to tell the architect, "You don't know what you're doing; I'm going to change the foundation." Likewise, it would be foolish for us to question our Great Architect, Jesus Christ.

Scripture contains a clear picture of the design of a strong foundation, and we need to know what it looks like, because the building is only as good as the foundation it stands on. Our lives can look so pretty on the outside, but what good are they if the foundation is bad? The storms that come into our lives reveal the strength of our foundation.

In order for us to embrace and fulfill God's purposes, we must have a strong foundation. Without a solid foundation, the four purposes previously discussed are impossible to apply to our own situations in the way that God desires.

Get Your Priorities Straight

Jesus told us, *"But seek first the Kingdom of God and His righteousness, and all these things shall be added to you"* (Matt. 6:33). As a minister, our first priority must be to seek and fulfill God's will. We accomplish this by daily putting all things in perspective, and by prioritizing our life according to what God says is important in order to fulfill His purposes in and through us. We must look to Him *daily* for strength to accomplish this task.

Do you think that God looks upon your kids as any less significant than He does upon the rest of the congregation of your church? Of course not! He looks at your children with the same love and concern as He does upon the one hundred, five hundred, or one thousand people in the congregation of your church; they are just as important and valuable to Him.

We would all agree that it is very important for our pastor to have a strong, intimate relationship with the Lord as a priority in his life. We would expect him to get up every day and spend time with the Lord, seeking Him for wisdom and guidance to lead his congregation, to be the right husband, and to be the best father that he can be. If he did not do that, we would not think him much of a pastor, because we know he needs God's empowerment and direction in order to lead.

We can easily put those expectations upon our pastor, but now let's look at ourselves. If God looks upon our children with no less significance, importance, and value than He does the whole congregation, then is it not just as important for us to be crawling up in God's lap every day, maintaining that strong foundation, that relationship with Christ to find the strength and wisdom we need to lead our families? I can tell you as a father of three, if I do not seek Christ every day, it does not take long before my old nature begins to come out. I need God's wisdom and direction, as all of us do.

When we look at families today, across the United States, we see that they are in trouble. Our kids are killing one another, abusing drugs, experimenting with sex, even within the body of Christ. I have been in family ministry as a counselor for over twenty years, and I have seen it all. In almost every situation, when there is a tragedy, a storm, one of the main reasons the family has gone amuck is because they have neglected these principles. They have not maintained a strong foundation.

Intimately Acquainted

In Deuteronomy 6, Moses gave instructions to God's people before going into the Promised Land. Within these instructions, God gives us His heart regarding how important it is for us to maintain this intimate relationship—this strong foundation.

> *Now this is the commandment, and these are the statutes and judgments which the LORD your God has commanded to teach you, that you may observe them in the land which you are crossing over to possess, that you may fear the LORD your God, to keep all His statutes and His commandments which I command you, you and your son and your grandson, all the days of your life, and that your days may be prolonged. Therefore hear, O Israel, and be careful to observe it, that it may be well with you, and that you may multiply greatly as the LORD God of your fathers has promised you—'a land flowing with milk and honey.' "Hear, O Israel: The LORD our God, the LORD is one! You shall love the LORD your God with all your heart, with all your soul, and with all your strength. And these words which I command you today shall be in your heart."*
>
> —Deuteronomy 6:1-6

Both verse three and verse four begin with, "*Hear, O Israel.*" What this means is that what follows is not incidental but is absolutely essential for the survival of Israel as a nation. Whenever we see that phrase repeated, the emphasis is, "Listen up." That is the emphasis God put on the following verses; He was saying it was essential to understand this principle, because without this Israel would die as a nation. What God said in Deuteronomy 6 is no exception to us today. The next few verses reveal the fundamental truth to the success of our job as ministers over our children.

In Deuteronomy 6:5, it says, *"Love the LORD your God with all your heart, with all your soul, and with all your strength."* This means that we must *choose* to have an intimate relationship with Him. Note the word "choose." Intimacy with Christ is a choice that you and I make every single day: closely acquainted, very familiar, and personal, abiding in Him. "With all your heart, soul and strength" means our total being, our whole body.

Verse six tells us God's words must be first in our hearts. In order for us to exemplify Christ and teach others, we must have God's Word within our own hearts. This means we must abide in Him, we must obey Him.

Our dependency upon Christ to help us fulfill this difficult task of raising kids is directly related to our relationship and intimacy with God.

Sadly, most people in the body of Christ have never been truly discipled in this truth. When you have not really been discipled and have never had someone more mature come alongside you to help you develop intimacy with the Lord, this type of intimate relationship can be difficult to understand. We are tempted to think: "How can one have an intimate relationship with Jesus Christ?"

Many think, "I go to church on Sunday. I'm a Christian: I prayed the prayer of salvation, I cried, I remember that day. What else is there? I quit smoking, I don't drink, and I'm a good person. Is there something more?" Yes, there is.

The Essential Ingredients

But why do you call Me "Lord, Lord," and not do the things which I say? Whoever comes to Me, and hears My sayings and does them, I will show you whom he is like: He is like a man building a house, who dug deep and laid the foundation on the rock. And when the flood arose, the stream beat vehemently against that house, and could not shake it, for it was founded on the rock. But he who heard and did nothing is like a man who built a house on the earth without a foundation, against which the stream beat vehemently; and immediately it fell. And the ruin of that house was great.

—Luke 6:46-49

There are three ingredients God gives us in these verses that describe a strong foundation. First, "comes to Me" means accepting Jesus Christ as your Lord and Savior. There must be a time in your life when you have sought forgiveness for your sins and asked Jesus Christ to come into your life as your

Lord and Savior. Merely being born in America and/or attending a church does not make you a Christian. It does not work that way.

Second, "hears My sayings" means abiding in Him, which describes our relationship to Christ.

The third ingredient He gives us is "does them." That means obeying or applying His Word in our lives.

Scripture tells us it is important to examine ourselves in each of these areas on an ongoing basis. *"Let us examine our ways, and test them, and let us return to the Lord"* (Lam. 3:40 NIV). So let's pretend I am an inspector coming to your house, and I am walking around pulling your carpets up and inspecting your foundation. Let's look at the following areas and inspect the three ingredients we learned in Luke 6:46-49.

The first test is either a "yes" or "no": has there been a time when you have asked Jesus Christ into your life as your Lord and Savior? This is the first ingredient God gives us for a strong foundation. You cannot skip this one. We must first be one of His kids. If you do not know what I am talking about, ask a pastor or Christian friend, "What does it mean?" If you're not sure, look up Romans 10:9-10 and pray this prayer:

Lord Jesus, I know that I am a sinner. I am sorry for my sin. Thank You for dying on the cross for me and paying the price for my sin. Please come into my heart. Fill me with Your Holy Spirit and help me to be Your disciple.

Thank You for forgiving me and coming into my life. Thank You that I am now a child of God and that I am going to heaven. Amen.

The next two ingredients deal with our abiding relationship and devotional life to Christ. First, our habits of prayer. Prayer is not a matter of attempting to alter external situations as much as what God wants to do inside our own hearts when we pray.

How is your prayer life? Is it growing daily? Do words like "intimate," "worship," and "listening" apply? Do the words "close relationship" describe it? Or is it more like speaking to a distant cousin? Do you pray as a husband and wife together every day? Do you pray with your children every day?

"Be anxious for nothing, but in everything by prayer and supplication, with thanksgiving, let your requests be made known to God" (Phil. 4:6). How is your prayer life? Give yourself a grade. What grade would you give it? Is there room for improvement?

Secondly, how often do you spend time reading and meditating upon the Word of God, only on Sunday morning at church? Perhaps your pastor is extraordinarily wise and a good teacher. Even so, if you are trying to live for a whole week on what he gives you on Sunday morning, you are definitely starving by the end of the week. Perhaps you drag yourself out for a midweek study as well; isn't that enough? Is it?

Many Christians put the *Daily Bread* booklets behind the toilet and try to kill two birds with one stone. They pull it out, read a little, and think, "OK,

I did my thing. I got into the Word today, praise the Lord." But by the time they get out the door, they have forgotten what they just read. Unfortunately, that is the way many treat the reading of the Word. We have so many opportunities with our CD players and the radio and so many other ways to get into the Word, but if we do not actively pursue this time alone with Christ and make sure it happens, and *choose* to meditate on His Word every single day, it won't happen.

Do you spend time meditating upon what you have read? When people hear the word *meditation,* some may think of it as a strange Hindu practice, but it is not. Meditation comes out of the Word of God. God wants us to meditate upon the things that we read. God wants us to spend time listening to what He is trying to teach us, to commune with us.

When my daughter Katie was nine, every time I came home, she ran up, put her arms around me, and would shout, "Daddy!" She'd give me a hug, and I'd get to kiss her. She is pretty tall now, but when she was younger, it was an even bigger production. She would run up, "Daddy!" and I would pick her up. She would sit on my arm as I walked into the house, and she would act like a princess, looking around, "See, Daddy loves me." She would sit in my arms for a few moments just to make sure her two older brothers would see her. Even today, it just blesses me so much when I walk into the house and she comes up and hugs me. I love it; I look forward to it every single day.

Now my teenage boys ... they do not even come downstairs when I get home. When I eventu-

ally see them, I get a, "Hey Dad," or just an unaffec-
tionate, "Hi Dad." Now . . . when they were younger,
however, those two little rug rats would run out and
climb on each leg as I walked into the house. The
next hour and a half we wrestled, and they would
not let me out of their sight. But as they grew up and
became mature, they began to take it for granted . . .
"Oh, Dad's going to come home. He always does."

I give you that illustration because we do the same
thing to the Lord. When we first came to Christ, we
could not wait to get into the Word. When we read
it, we knew God was speaking right to our hearts.
Oftentimes we experienced wonderful emotions, and
when we read His Word, if it did not minister to us,
we knew ten people to whom it would minister. "Oh,
gosh, I've got to call my sister, she needs this!" We
were so excited!

But as we grow in the Lord and we begin to
mature, our attitude becomes, "Yeah, yeah, Matthew
again." It becomes stale. Sadly, we no longer have the
attitude of "Daddy's here!" We cannot let this become
stale. Just think about this: we have the blessed privilege to go into the Holy of Holies and crawl in His
lap, to hear Him whisper awesome truths to us, and
tell us how wonderful and important we are to Him!
When was the last time you delved into the Word
expecting Him to speak to you; has it become stale?

The first thing recorded in the Bible after Jesus
Christ gave up His spirit on the cross is that He
ripped the veil, top to bottom. That was recorded to
remind us that Christ died not only for our sins, but
also so we would have relationship with Him, now.

He is not waiting until we get to Heaven; He wants us to have intimacy with Him *now*. Unfortunately, we get into these stale routines and forget this very important principle regarding our daily relationship to Christ.

As a daddy, when my kids come up and want to be with me, and they say something nice, I am so blessed. Do you think God is any different? He loves it when you and I call "time out" and say, "Daddy, this is Your time, mine and Yours, right now, and I'm not going to let my busyness get in the way. I'm going to maintain this, God."

However, do you find it interesting that every time we try to start this daily abiding relationship with Christ, all the distractions seem to come? Isn't that amazing? Your mind gets flooded with thoughts . . . the bills, your spouse, your kids, etc.

Satan sends those distractions because he knows the purpose of the blood in our veins and the air in our lungs is not to be "good people," not to be the best mommy or best daddy, best husband or wife, but to have a relationship with Christ. Everything stems out of this relationship.

Everything, especially our power to do our ministry as a parent, comes from this intimacy, this daily abiding relationship with Christ. Mark 4:34 says, *". . . And when they were alone, He explained all things to His disciples."* Some of the greatest mysteries that I have learned as a minister, as a pastor, as a father, as a husband are when I was spending time with Jesus in my daily devotional and reading Scripture.

I am nothing special; I am no more special than you are. God loves us each the same, and He longs to communicate to us. There is no parenting book written that will cover every situation that you and I will face. That is why God wants us to depend on Him each day, to look to His Word to give us understanding and teach us our purposes; and if we follow them, He will guide us and empower us.

Many times He wants to speak to us, to give us the wisdom we need in order to deal with our situations, yet we are too busy to spend that time with Him. If we do not exhort ourselves on an ongoing basis in this area, our relationship soon becomes stale.

*"**Study** to show thyself approved unto God, a workman that needeth not to be ashamed, rightly dividing the Word of truth"* (2 Tim. 2:15 KJV). How well are you handling the Word of God? Again, give yourself a grade.

Obedience Is Better Than Sacrifice

First, do you trust God with your finances; do you tithe? Proverbs 3:9-10 says, *"Honor the LORD with your possessions, and with the firstfruits of all your increase; so your barns will be filled with plenty, and your vats will overflow with new wine."* Some people may wonder, "What does tithing have to do with raising kids?" It is simply this, if we truly want all of God's grace, power, and wisdom to raise our kids, we must trust Him with what He has given us.

We cannot ask God for everything, and then say, "Well, God, I know what You have asked me to do, but . . ." Sadly, less than 10 percent of the body of

Christ tithe regularly, and definitely do not use God's Word regarding what to give and how much[1]. We want all of God's blessing, but are we ready to trust Him in our finances? God wants to bless us, but there are some things about which He has said, "Trust Me." There are things that He wants us to do, and this is one of them. Tithing is not a salvation issue; it is a trust issue with Christ. Give yourself a grade in this area as well.

Next, where do your priorities lie between God, spouse, children, work, church, leisure time, and fellowship? Are they in proper order, and does your family concur? I have counseled many people who are in ministry over the years. Many of their homes are not in order, and they are suffering for it. Unfortunately, these people do not have their priorities straight.

God shares His heart regarding our priorities in 1 Timothy 3:1-13. I encourage you to take these Scripture passages and spend some time going through them. It is clear that your home must be your first priority in order for you to be a good minister. Many homes are out of order; many people are spending more time in leisure or work, or even in their church and their ministry, outside their own family. Give yourself a grade in this area.

Finally, are you practicing godly principles in your home? ". . . *Love, joy, peace, patience, kindness, goodness, faithfulness, gentleness, self-control"* (Gal. 5:22-23 NIV)—are those the things your children are seeing growing and improving in your home? What is it that they are seeing? Give yourself a grade.

What is most important to you, other than your relationship with Christ? If anything else becomes more important, you will suffer and so will your family. God blesses obedience. Disobedience, on the other hand, puts us outside God's grace (though not of salvation) and causes us to begin to operate in our flesh.

Do you see any room for improvement? These are not trick questions. God gave us these instructions, and He made it pretty clear for us to understand. He said that we must encourage each other in an ongoing basis in these areas. Just like you, I need God's power and His grace every single day. *But we must never forget that God will not do by miracle what He has called you to do by obedience.*

Let's identify the most significant aspect for building our foundation—intimacy with Christ.

The Corner Stone

If we are to build a strong foundation, we must first ensure that we have chosen the proper cornerstone. Intimacy, abiding in Christ, is that on which our foundation must be built.

There is significance to the order: accept Jesus Christ, abide and obey. Most Christians concentrate all their energy on the third one, "Oh, I've got to quit doing this, I'm just such a sinner, I can't stop." Fortunately, a byproduct of *abiding* is the power to obey.

When people come in for counseling, struggling with sins—sex, pornography, drinking, or whatever—the first question I ask is, "How's your abiding relationship to Christ?"

Most of them ask me, "What's that?"

I explain, "It's the connection that gives you the power to obey."

Our intimacy with God is what gives us the power, the grace for that day to have victory over sin. And He only gives us grace for the day. He does not give us grace for a week; He gives us grace and power for the day. We need to see this connection and understand this spiritual principle.

Our devotional life is so like a foundation under a house. You cannot see it, for it is under the dirt and covered up by flooring and carpet. But the results will be obvious as the storms touch our lives. We usually are more apt to spend most of our time and money on the things on the outside of our home that make it look nice. Typically, our concerns are for our own pleasure or how others may see us. But it is the foundation that holds the house up, not the things people can see.

In the following chapters, I will give you some good, practical, biblical tools to help you raise your kids. But if you skip this one, if you ignore your foundation, you are going to go right back to your old habits. If our vertical axis is out of whack, every horizontal relationship will be negatively affected.

Rebellion in Me

When you hear the word *rebellion,* what comes to mind? Teenagers? The word *rebellion* often is associated with adolescents. However, *rebellion* does not apply solely to teenagers. It means *any* resistance to authority[2]. When we choose to do things our own way, or to reprioritize our lives according to what is most important to us, not God; when we do not maintain a daily, close, intimate relationship with the Lord, we are in rebellion.

Intimacy and abiding in Him are choices, but God clearly tells us in Scripture, "Do it." As He said in Deuteronomy to His children before they went into the Promised Land, "Listen up. This is all-important: Love God with all your heart, mind, body and soul" (Deut. 6:1-6). You and I must choose every day to maintain this intimate relationship with Christ.

The erosion of our spiritual foundation begins with neglect. How can we combat our natural tendency toward apathy? The answer is we must train ourselves. What are your first thoughts in the morning? When you are lying in bed, when you become conscious, what is your first thought? Train yourself this way: first thing in the morning—focus your mind on Christ and remember or acknowledge to yourself and God how depraved you are. The great thing is God already knows. And despite your depravity, He says, "Here I am; I want to bless you."

God knows everything about us. He knows how weak and foolish and angry we are. He knew all the "junk" that we had inside of us when we came to be one of His kids; He knew, *and He chose us anyway*! He is not there to condemn us; He is there to bless us.

We must train our minds. Our first thoughts in the morning should be, "God here I am. Thank you that I am one of Yours! I know there are so many areas in my life that need improvement; God, I need Your strength!" The Lord is longing to hear you say that every day.

Train yourself to put your mind upon the cross in the first moments of the morning; not on your bills, your spouse, your kids, or your job, no matter how pressing those things may seem. Pray and ask Him for His grace to love your family and to walk in His will today. Now, this is before you begin or do your personal devotional time with Him.

"Do not be deceived, God is not mocked; for whatever a man sows, that he will also reap" (Gal. 6:7). If we put God first, before all things, He will respond.

God Is Sovereign

As God's children and His ministers, we must always remember that God is in control, and He has a purpose in the trials that we face. Psalm 139:1-18 tells us our days are predestined, every single one of them. They were written in His book before time was created, before the earth even existed. Every single one of your days God has predestined. He is in control.

"For we are His workmanship, created in Christ Jesus for good works, which God prepared beforehand that we should walk in them" (Eph. 2:10). We can take comfort in the knowledge that in every situation, God has already been there. He knows all things; He is never surprised. So when you get up Saturday morning to find your three-year-old has spilled orange juice and cereal all over the floor

and is making a little goulash, you can walk in and calmly say, "OK, God, You were already here. What is this about?" And on Friday night when your teenager comes home an hour and a half later than he was supposed to, you can remind yourself, "OK, God, You have been here already. You knew this was going to happen to me. You said in all situations You have prepared me for good works." We can glorify Christ in all our circumstances!

Here is a catchy phrase I once heard that you can write down. I don't know who the original author is, but it has been a good reminder for me over the years. "If I put my eyes on others, I get stressed. If I put my eyes on myself, I get depressed. If I put my eyes on Jesus, I get blessed." Post that on your refrigerator or on your mirror in the morning!

Remember: Our Transformation

Again, our first purpose as parents is our transformation. God has a plan and purpose in the trials that we face as parents and ministers. It is His desire that we become more like Him, and He often uses the difficult trials that come our way as agents of our transformation.

> *My brethren, count it all joy when you fall into various trials, knowing that the testing of your faith produces patience. But let patience have its perfect work, that you may be perfect and complete, lacking nothing.*
> —James 1:2-4

> *But whoever keeps His word, truly the love of*
> *God is perfected in him. By this we know that*
> *we are in Him.*
>
> —1 John 2:5

Matthew 14:22-31a is a perfect illustration of this process. In this passage of Scripture, Jesus was ministering to people all day long. He fed thousands, He healed and preached, and at the end of the day, He was exhausted. He walked down to the Sea of Galilee and told the apostles, "Get in the boat, go to the other side; I'll meet you over there." So the apostles jumped in the boat and began to sail across.

When they were halfway across the sea, a storm came up. This storm was so fierce that the apostles were afraid for their lives; they were afraid of drowning in the violent waves. Keep in mind: most of these men were experienced fishermen, so we can only imagine the intensity of that storm. But Jesus had sent His disciples out into that storm, knowing full well it was coming. He purposefully put them out there, just like He often does to us. And the very thing that the apostles were most afraid of, the water, Jesus walked upon. Of the thing they feared the most, Jesus proclaimed, "I am more powerful than that."

Seeing Jesus, Peter cried, "Jesus, it's You!" and stepped out of the boat. He actually walked on water! But then he took his eyes off Jesus for a few moments, put them back on the storm, and began to sink. We do not actually know how far under Peter went. But at some point, He cried out for help. And Jesus did not make him flounder there, He immediately pulled him up, the moment he cried out.

So often as parents in crises we take our eyes off of Christ and His promises, and we put them on the circumstances, and those circumstances overwhelm us. And so many times, Jesus is the last person we cry out to. But God *wants* to prove Himself faithful and more powerful than our circumstances! We must fix our eyes upon Him and remember He sends us into storms because He has a plan.

Just as God showed His power above the elements when He walked upon water, just as He glorified Himself and proved Himself more powerful than the apostles' greatest fear, God wants to do the same thing for us as we raise up our children. As Christian parents, we need to live each day before God and seek to please Him alone, keeping our eyes on Him, not on the storms and the difficulties. Sadly, because we do not have intimacy with Christ, our peace is often quenched by the difficulties in raising our children. We are easily agitated and angered; the last thing we experience is joy and strength over the things that come our way.

"Yet if anyone suffers as a Christian, let him not be ashamed, but let him glorify God in this matter" (1 Pet. 4:16). No one enjoys suffering, but for parents, it is part of the job. Rather than ask, "Why, God? Why is this happening to me?" the question should be, "What? What are You revealing in me through this circumstance, God?"

Suffering is part of God's plan. God wills and commands the situations around us for our inner

73

transformation and for His glorification. If we are not totally dependent upon His daily strength, His wisdom in every situation, the temptation is to depend upon ourselves. However, the moment we begin to depend upon ourselves rather than God, our sin nature appears. These fleshly reactions and attitudes do not reflect His promises. This happens most often when we are out of fellowship, or if we reject the fact that God uses our children to bring about our inner transformation.

> *No temptation has overtaken you except such as is common to man; but God is faithful, who will not allow you to be tempted beyond what you are able, but with the temptation will also make the way of escape, that you may be able to bear it.*
>
> —1 Corinthians 10:13

In Christ, no trial is beyond our ability to triumph over. God is not saying that you and I must be perfect. God uses even our failures to help our children grow! We do not have to be perfect, but we must be changing, growing, maturing in Christ. We must receive and accept this truth and be responsible for our actions. The moment that you and I accepted Jesus Christ as Savior, the journey began. We will travel this journey of transformation until we die. There will never be a place where we say, "OK, we're done", until we are with Him in heaven.

Don't Labor in Vain

"Unless the LORD builds the house, they labor in vain who build it; unless the LORD guards the city, the watchman stays awake in vain" (Ps. 127:1). God so wants to protect our families, He wants to intercede in our kids' lives. He wants to show Himself faithful and powerful, but we must first allow Him to be the Lord over our family.

God's Word tells us that He blesses obedience. When we are disobedient in the areas of intimacy and relationship with Christ, God cannot intercede on our behalf, even if we want Him to. He wants to show Himself faithful, but we need to do our part. In order for us to glorify Him, we must be intimate with Him each day, and then we will experience transformation and stand on a solid foundation. *Remember*, God will not do by miracle what He has called you to do by obedience.

As a parent, as a minister of Christ, the mainspring of our service is not our love for our children, but our love for Jesus Christ. If we are devoted to the cause of our children, we shall soon be discouraged and broken hearted, for we will often meet with more ingratitude from our children than we would from our dog. But if our motive is our love and service to God, no ingratitude can hinder us from serving our children and fulfilling His will and wishes.

The method is never the key to accomplishing God's purposes. The key is our relationship with Him. God will foil the best of man's plans if He is left out of them. The tools we will cover in the remainder of this book will be extremely useful in helping you raise your kids. But the tools are not the key. This is the key: not the plan, but the relationship.

The integrity of the foundation on which we raise our children is directly related to the strength of our relationship with Jesus Christ, and to our daily dependence upon Him. Our intimacy with God through prayer and reading and making Scripture part of our daily lives will transform our hearts to become willing servants to our children. We must be disciplined; we must be devoted.

There is a glorious promise to God's children in 2 Peter 1:1-4.

> *To those who have obtained like precious faith with us by the righteousness of our God and Savior Jesus Christ: grace and peace be multiplied to you in the knowledge of God and of Jesus our Lord, as His divine power has given to us all things that pertain to life and godliness, through the knowledge of Him who called us by glory and virtue, by which have been given to us exceedingly great and precious promises, that through these you may be partakers of the divine nature, having escaped the corruption that is in the world through lust.*

If you could get up every morning and take a pill that would give you peace, knowledge, divine power, and wisdom that would guide you in every situation of the day, would you take it? Clearly, that is what God promises us if we will but seek Him.

So I say to you, ask, and it will be given to you; seek, and you will find; knock, and it will be opened to you. For everyone who asks receives, and he who seeks finds, and to him who knocks it will be opened. If a son asks for bread from any father among you, will he give him a stone? Or if he asks for a fish, will he give him a serpent instead of a fish? Or if he asks for an egg, will he offer him a scorpion? If you then, being evil, know how to give good gifts to your children, how much more will your heavenly Father give the Holy Spirit to those who ask Him!

—Luke 11:9-13

To help you better understand this all-important truth—when Jesus Christ died on the cross, He made a deposit of grace, power, and wisdom in each one of our names. In that deposit there is grace, mercy, power, wisdom, and knowledge to accomplish every task He puts before you. Intimacy with Him is the only way to make a withdrawal from that account. Satan knows this, and that is why it has been so difficult for many of you. It seems as though every time you made a commitment to have a good devotional life, every time you committed to get alone with the Lord even for only ten or fifteen minutes, soon the distractions of the world and all its requirements robbed you. And you lost that intimacy.

Start Building

If God has revealed to you that your relationship with Him has become stale, the first thing that you need to do is ask Him to forgive you. Tell Him, "Father, I'm sorry. I forgot. I've lost my first love. I've allowed the important things I do every day to become more important than the reason I exist; to have fellowship with You."

Secondly, commit to begin anew; yet be sure it is a reasonable commitment. Do not overdo it. Start with fifteen minutes; tell yourself you are going to read one chapter, just one. Then read that chapter with the expectation that God is waiting to speak to your heart. When you are finished, meditate for a few moments on what you have read.

Finally, get a journal. When you keep a journal in your devotional time, you are telling yourself and the Lord, "I'm expecting You to say something to me today." This is very important. Wait upon the Lord, and whatever He gives you, write it down and date it. He may give you direction or a prayer, or simply remind you of His promises.

Personally, I have reams of paper that I have kept over the years. When I am going through a trial, thinking, "God, what's going on?" I go back, and I start reading through my journal. Usually by the third or fourth page, I am brought to tears because of the things written there that God spoke to me about my life, my kids, my wife, and for the ministry.

Intimacy is a process. Begin with fifteen minutes a day, and it will grow. You will learn how to abide in Christ and to pray without ceasing. You will learn how to be in fellowship with Him throughout the day. And on this strong foundation, you will be able to build a solid family.

---

[1] Barna Identifies Seven Paradoxes Regarding America's Faith, The Barna Group, December 17, 2002

[2] Webster's New International Dictionary of the English Language; Second Edition Unabridged; G & C Merriam Company, Publishers, Springfield, MA 1944

Chapter Four

Love Them

Surprisingly, as a family counselor I hear many kids make the statement, *"My parents don't love me."* over and over again, despite the fact that virtually any parent questioned would emphatically state that they *do,* in fact, love their kids. Unfortunately, the truth is that parents sometimes *act like* they do not love their kids. The frustration and difficulties of parenting can bring out the worst in us, and we do things that are perceived as the opposite of love. Over time, these perceptions become reality and our children truly are *unloved,* for all intents and purposes.

Therefore, it is essential that we learn to show love to our children. The good news is, if our foundation of intimacy with Jesus Christ has been properly laid, we are capable, in God's strength, of building the "supports of love" that our children need.

Each Child Is Unique

An important principle we often forget to consider is that God *uniquely* creates each child. My daughter, Katie, for instance, is very shy; you might say she has a tendency towards a phobic personality. From the time she was able to walk, up until she was about five years old, if we were in a public place, anywhere away from the house, she had to be physically holding on to either my wife or me. She would not leave our sides. Thankfully, now that Katie is older, she is much more confident. We live next door to my brother, who has five very energetic children, and that has been the greatest therapy for Katie. She has definitely progressed.

But when she was younger, even at church where she knew so many people, she was extremely shy. She would see her mom standing a mere ten feet away during fellowship time and would kind of pull away from me, then *run* over to where her mom was. It was a little weird.

On Fridays, when Katie was in kindergarten, they had praise and worship for the whole school, about three or four hundred students. Fridays were definitely very difficult days! Each week when worship started, with all these kids screaming, "Oh, praise the Lord," it was like a nightmare for Katie. She would cover her ears and put her head down. It was fearful for her.

Even the daily routine on the playground with fifty kids throwing balls around and yelling was too much for Katie. So she would sit at the table, by herself, and color and talk with the teachers. When we went to Disneyland, it was anything but the "happiest place on earth." Katie did not like it at all. It would be almost 5:00 in the afternoon before she could even relax with all those people around. That is just the way Katie was.

Yet my boys were completely different. They were nothing like Katie. Nick, in particular, was the complete opposite. We had to chase him around all the time, "Get over here young man!" He always wanted to be so independent.

Many friends and family members noticed Katie's behavior; it seemed strange to them. What if my wife and I, when my daughter was behaving fearfully, ignored her needs and instead said, "Will you stop it? Let go of me! Stand over there. The boys never did this." What if we had started shunning her? What would have happened to her? We would have hurt her and possibly caused long-lasting effects, simply because we refused to adapt to her unique emotional needs.

Each of our kids are unique! All of our kids are very different; each of them has different emotional needs. In order to love them, we need to become students of our children and learn how to adjust or adapt to their personalities. We need to know what our children need, how to adjust the way we communicate with them, and how to show affection to them—each one very differently. If we do not do that, serious problems can occur.

Many parents, without knowing or recognizing it, are destroying their children's spirits and damaging their self-worth. By misrepresenting the Lord, by not loving their children and meeting their emotional needs, these parents also are prematurely eroding their own influential power over their children.

Love Takes Time

Another important key to love is spending time with our children. In today's world we are being pulled in so many different directions—our jobs, our ministries, our hobbies—that we may leave little or no time for our children. Even those parents whose kids are in soccer or softball or other sports are at risk. Sports are good, but some people have taken them to the extreme. If you have one child who is a sports "nut," but the other three are not, what are you communicating to those three when you spend all day Saturday and Sunday like a taxi cab driving the "sport" around while they stay home? Or worse yet, when you drag them along and make them sit in the bleachers. We must find a balanced way to love each of our kids and enjoy what they like to do.

Today, in our society, many women who are married work. Please understand, however, I am not putting down working moms. If you want to live in Southern California where I am, you almost have to have two incomes. There is no question about it. But the key is, when those working parents come home, where are their hearts and minds? Many of us who work, when we get home what is foremost in our minds is, "Kids, leave me alone for a while. I need my space." We are not available for them, and therein lies the problem.

Loving our kids is not necessarily affected by the fact that we are working, but by our behavior and attitude when we are home with them. Today, an average working mother spends eleven minutes a day in one-on-one communication with her child. For those with multiple children, that time per child decreases even further. On an entire weekend, a working mom spends about thirty minutes per day in one-on-one communication with her child. A father today spends about eight minutes a day communicating one-on-one with his child, and about fourteen total minutes of one-on-one communication with his kids on a weekend[1].

Within these same statistics, we find that children today are watching between three and four hours of TV a day. Is it any wonder that the media is proselytizing and infecting our children's minds with worldly views? Loving our kids and meeting their emotional needs means sacrifice, giving of ourselves and being available for them, adapting to their interests, be it reading a book to them or playing catch. It takes time.

The Most Powerful Motivator

It is my observation through study that there are four basic forces that motivate all humans. First is love, the most powerful motivator. The second is physical needs: food, security, warmth. Number three is pleasure: our jobs, our car, our house . . . things that please us. Fourth, and least powerful, is pain and fear.

As parents, when it comes to trying to motivate our children, we lean most heavily on pain and fear. Isn't that interesting? The reality is, however, that a far more powerful motivator is love. Love is what is going to help our children when they are not with us, as they grow and become adolescents. Love is going to be the most powerful motivator to get them to say, "No, I don't want that" or "I won't do that." Our love for them is the key. What was the motivation that caused Jesus to come down and die for us? John 3:16 tells us it was His love for us that motivated Him to die on the cross.

React in the Flesh (Sin) or Respond in Love (Truth)

The dictionary says *to react* means "to act in response to a stimulant or to stimulus, to act in opposition[2]." So to react is a **negative** action. Loving someone is not *reacting* to that person.

As Christian parents, as ministers, we should only be negative regarding sin and the misrepresentation of God. We should not be negatively reacting to our children in any circumstance.

Reacting takes no thought. It is a "no-brainer," in which our mind reacts in the flesh. In other words, whatever comes to mind, we simply react to it. Reacting requires no self-control. It is our sin nature, our flesh. When their kids do something wrong, many parents will react in the wrong way with the first thing that comes to their minds if they allow their flesh to dictate; things like yelling, being angry, harsh words, or angry and disgusted facial expressions. The list of sinful and fleshly reactionary expressions toward our children can get pretty long.

It is so important that we remember *every day* that we are the most powerful influences in our children's lives! Every time we get angry and react to our kids in a negative way, we should visualize pulling a sword out and slicing their hearts; every single time. Of course we do not see the damage we cause in the physical sense, but it is truly taking place. In addition, when we do not deal with that damage properly, infection sets in, then bitterness, then resentment; and when our kids become teenagers, we pay the price.

As a counselor, I have seen hundreds of Christian boys and girls with broken hearts. They are so infected, so full of pain, and sadly, the parents who raised these kids never even considered the damage they were doing to their children over and over again by reacting to their behavior instead of responding in love.

Reaction to circumstances and our emotions takes no time; it is instantaneous. Proverbs 15:1 tells us, *". . . a harsh word stirs up anger."* The Bible also tells us that we are to remove things like harsh words from our behavior. *"But now you yourselves are to put off all these: anger, wrath, malice, blasphemy, filthy language out of your mouth"* (Col. 3:8). We are to accept this truth and make a conscious decision to stop any sinful reaction towards our children. Sadly, it is quite common for Christian parents to react in the flesh towards their children, yet never take responsibility for the results.

According to the dictionary, *to respond* means "to react positive[3]." In other words, responding is **positive**, contrary to reacting. Responding takes *thought;* we have to use our mind and will. Scripture commands that we "*. . . bring every thought captive unto God's Word*" (2 Cor. 10:5). Responding also takes *self-control.* We must bring our will under subjection to the power of God, which allows the fruits of the Holy Spirit to blossom, one of which is self-control. "*But the fruit of the Spirit is love, joy, peace, longsuffering, kindness, goodness, faithfulness, gentleness, self-control*" (Gal. 5:22-23). In addition, Scripture tells us we must add self-control to our foundation of faith:

> *But also for this very reason, giving all diligence, add to your faith virtue, to virtue knowledge, to knowledge self-control, to self-control perseverance, to perseverance godliness, to godliness brotherly kindness, and to brotherly kindness love.*
>
> —2 Peter 1:5-7

Finally, responding rather than reacting takes *time.* It may take as long as counting to ten, it may take much longer. In a later chapter we will discuss discipline, including the importance of never doing it in anger—sometimes the ability to respond with appropriate discipline hinges on taking a time out for parents.

"*The heart of the righteous studies how to answer . . .*" (Prov. 15:28).

"So then, my beloved brethren, let every man be swift to hear, slow to speak, slow to wrath; for the wrath of man does not produce the righteousness of God" (James 1:19-20).

Clearly, Scripture instructs that we are not to react in the flesh; we are to respond in love thoughtfully. Remember, our purpose is to glorify God, and that means even during discipline, even when our kids are failing, even when they do not want to listen, even when they are challenging us . . . even then, we need to respond in love. Because, ultimately, it is His will, not ours.

The Strong-Willed Child

Proverbs 14:29 says, *"He who is slow to wrath has great understanding, but he who is impulsive exalts folly."* In other words, reacting rather than responding encourages and motivates the folly of continuous childish behavior in our children. This is especially true in strong-willed children.

As I shared previously, during the first four or five years of my oldest son's life, I frequently reacted to his strong-willed behavior like a raving maniac. I was angry, and I abused my authority. Finally God asked me, "Hey Craig, would you ever put gasoline on a fire when you're trying to put it out?"

"Of course not."

"Well every time you get angry and your son knows it, you are provoking him to continuous folly in his behavior."

Scripture reveals that when we push their buttons, strong-willed kids are going to push us right back.

That is the way God wired them. Those strong wills are the Peter's and Paul's of the world. We need people like them in our lives, in the kingdom! They are those who, when they are trained right, face the offer of drugs with, "Hey, no way man, get this stuff out of my face!"

We are to respond in truth, not driven by our feelings and emotions. *In truth* means that our response is a result of a heart and conscience informed with the Word. Again, it goes back to our foundation.

"Cursed is the one who does not confirm all the words of this law by observing them. And all the people shall say, 'Amen!'" (Deut. 27:26). *To confirm* means God's Word has come into our hearts and dictates our behavior. We are to respond in love.

> *"Teacher, which is the great commandment in the law?"*
> *Jesus said to him, "'You shall love the LORD your God with all your heart, with all your soul, and with all your mind.' This is the first and great commandment. And the second is like it: 'You shall love your neighbor as yourself.'"*
> —Matthew 22:36-39

In this passage God has indicated the importance of love and the value of human life. When we love and value someone, we treat them accordingly. Obviously, we can choose to respond and react in the opposite of love towards anyone, even our children, to whom we are called to minister to and exemplify Christ.

Here is an example of acting in the opposite of love; many of us have experienced a similar scenario. It is a heated moment after your child just did something really foolish, and the two of you are in the midst of an intense debate. Then the phone rings, and you stop to answer (it's a friend of yours): "Hello. Hi, oh yeah, everything's OK. I'm fine, how are you?" You seem happy to hear from them and your tone of voice is very pleasant instantly after you picked up the phone. What did you just communicate to your child? The person on the phone is more valuable than him or her.

Sadly, we frequently do that, never even thinking twice about it. Especially when our kids are little, before their cognitive skills are developed, they see it so plainly: "Mom or Dad honors or values that person more than they value me." One reason we find so many kids struggling with self-worth today is because this behavior is a common practice within the home, even in Christian homes.

Love Is a Choice

The Bible says that we are to "put on love." It is a *choice*, not a *feeling*. *"But above all these things put on love, which is the bond of perfection"* (Col. 3:14). The word translated "love" here is *agape*. *The Nelson Illustrated Bible Dictionary* says this about *agape love:* "contrary to a popular understanding, the significance of 'agape' is not that it is unconditional love, but that it is primarily a love of the *will* rather than of the *emotion.*"

Agape love means responding to my children as if I care and they are very valuable, even when, in reality, I may not care. I may be thinking negative thoughts, but I respond with love and patience. I have learned self-control, the art of quenching my flesh, so that I avoid saying something foolish, something judgmental, mean, or unkind. This is the fruit of the Spirit, not the fruit of Craig. This type of love does not come naturally. It is not a feeling; it is a choice, yielding to the Holy Spirit. Love is the decision to put value on another person. Romans 13:8 says, *"Owe no one anything except to love one another, for he who loves another has fulfilled the law."*

Communicating love starts with the heart. Learning to respond in love rather than react from the flesh is a process. Today, I no longer react in anger to my children but respond in love. Praise God, my oldest son has not held any un-forgiveness toward me for the many mistakes during his first six years of life. It is because God has healed any memory of anger and sinful behavior from me.

If you are trapped in a reactive pattern of behavior, take heart. You and your child can experience similar healing. In the next chapter we will deal with changing that reactive behavior to loving response. It is important to understand, however, if we choose to continue reacting negatively to our children, we will pay dearly.

[1] http://www.findarticles.com/p/articles/mi_m1175/is_v20/ai_4433362

[2] *Webster's New International Dictionary of the English Language; Second Edition Unabridged*; G & C Merriam Company, Publishers, Springfield, MA 1944

[3] *Webster's II New Riverside Dictionary Revised Edition, Office Edition*, Houghton Mifflin Company, 1996

CHAPTER FIVE

Love Is?

All of us believe that we really do love our children. But the only way we can truly know is by
comparing what we think love is against what God's
Word tells us it is. To understand "love" truly, there
is no better passage we can read than 1 Corinthians
13, which breaks down and describes just what love
is and what love is not. So in this chapter we will
examine what God's Word says love is, and what it is
not; let's evaluate ourselves.

However, before we do so, please keep something
in mind as we go through this process. The enemy
very much enjoys bringing condemnation onto us.
Do not let him do that! Yes, the Holy Spirit will bring
conviction in areas we need to shore up, and our job
is to receive that conviction. But we are not to feel
condemned, because we are not condemned. *There is
no condemnation in Christ* (Rom. 8:1).

Think about this: there is a reason that you are
reading this material right now. God has been waiting
until this specific moment to share these things with

95

you. Tell Him, "OK, God, I am ready. As You reveal these things to me, if I am doing something wrong in this area, I pray that You would bring conviction, and I would desire to change."

As we read 1 Corinthians 13, notice that all the terms describing love are verbs outwardly observed, not adjectives. This is because agape love can only be described by observing it in action. Love is not something that we can merely *define;* it is something that we *do*. It is not a feeling or an attitude; it is an action that always relates to someone else, never to self.

> *Love suffers long and is kind; love does not envy; love does not parade itself, is not puffed up; does not behave rudely, does not seek its own, is not provoked, thinks no evil; does not rejoice in iniquity, but rejoices in the truth; bears all things, believes all things, hopes all things, endures all things. Love never fails..*
> —1 Corinthians 13:4-8a

Let's look at each of these separately. In order to evaluate ourselves regarding our love for our children, it is helpful to look at those characteristics which are the opposite of love.

More Patience

The opposite of long-suffering is *impatience*. **Love is not impatient**. When we put selfish or unrealistic expectations on our children, we are not loving them. I hear parents complain, "My three-year old constantly leaves messes, and doesn't want to obey."

My response: "Really? What do you expect of a three-year old?"

Others complain, "My teenager never wants to do their chores!"

I respond by asking, "Is that a surprise?"

"Well, he's in the 99th percentile."

"How have you trained him?"

Then parents say, "What do you mean, 'trained him?' I just expect him to do it."

I say, "Oh really? Well, that's your problem then. No wonder he's fourteen and acts like he's six, because you place expectations on him, yet you have no idea how to train him to meet those expectations. Your anger and exasperation have merely continued the folly in his behavior. Who's really to blame, your fourteen-year old, or you?"

Our love for our kids *must* be long-suffering. Whether it is the "terrible twos" or the "terrible teens," love is hard work. The minute our children come home from the hospital, they just *want, want, want*. Everything is, "Mine, mine, mine." But we cannot be impatient! Love requires patience.

Keep in mind, some children will require much more patience than others. My son Nicholas was a mule! He required so much time from my wife and me, and ten times the amount of energy compared to my son Justin and daughter Katie. It was constant! He would wake up in the morning, and by 9:00 am my wife and I would think, "Oh my gosh, he's beating to a drum, but it sure is not ours." Sometimes we would have to discipline him twenty, even thirty times in one day. Justin or Katie, meanwhile, might have required one or two disciplines.

Loving Nicholas was indeed hard work! Often our thoughts were, "I'm sick of this! Why can't he just obey the rules? Why doesn't he just grow up?" We would stay up until all hours of the night discussing him: "Oh, gosh, what are we going to do tomorrow? God give us strength!" Loving Nicholas required a tremendous amount of patience.

I want to say something briefly at this point about attention deficit disorder (ADD). ADD is a genuine disorder, which causes an inability to focus, take direction, put commands in order, respond, and so on[1]. I do work with some children who truly have ADD or attention deficit/hyperactivity disorder (ADHD), but I would venture to say that over 85 percent of the ADD and ADHD diagnoses today are false and misdiagnosed. This is especially obvious when I consider the questions the therapist or physician typically asks the parents about their child's behavior, while never asking about the parents' method of training. In addition, they never consider how many times the parents are reacting to their child with anger, exasperating his/her behavior to continuous folly.

I often wonder why so many kids are diagnosed with ADD or ADHD. Mainly it seems that they did not want to sit in class and listen to the teacher, or have had zero training at home other than yelling and screaming. With no consistent loving discipline, it is no wonder they act the way they do. I have told many parents, "It's not that your child has ADD or ADHD

. . . but it's your ignorance and unwillingness to love and train your child according to God's will."

When parents are blessed with a strong-willed child, they often believe something is wrong with that child, but the only problem is their unwilling-ness to yield and obey. We call this disorder *UADD,* or unwilling attention deficit disorder. If they do not have UADD, then it is *LOPD,* lack of parenting disorder, or a combination of both.

If your child has been diagnosed with ADD or ADHD, however, please do not think you must imme-diately take them off of their medication. Instead, apply the things that you are learning through this book. You might find that ninety days from now, you will be able to wean them off that medication, and perhaps you will discover he/she never needed it in the first place. We have witnessed this many times. I encourage you to pray about that.

Discipline With a Smile

Love is . . . kind. The opposite of kindness is being unkind. ***Love is not unkind.*** Unkindness is allowing ourselves to be provoked, getting angry, yelling, judging, comparing our children to their siblings, and acting as if their failures are a threat against our parental authority.

We must remember that our homes are a training ground. Our kids are born without character. They do not have traits of maturity. The Word tells us that foolishness is bound up in their hearts.

Why do we act surprised by their behavior? It seems that we think if we are not angry, our discipline will not work. Many parents were raised in this way, so we are just repeating what we learned. That is the way I was raised. I believed if I wasn't twisting my face and raising my voice, my discipline was not working. However, where is that behavior commended in the Bible? Nowhere. We must learn how to discipline with no sinful expression, without our hair standing up or our veins popping out of our neck. The good news is when we submit to the Lord, we will be able to do it.

The sad reality is that in many Christian homes, parents show more contempt and more unkindness toward their own children than they do anyone else on earth—reacting in the flesh instead of responding in love (truth). We must train ourselves to be kind. *"Be kindly affectionate to one another with brotherly love, in honor giving preference to one another"* (Rom. 12:10).

Encouragement, Not Envy

Love does not envy. Parental jealousy or envy can result when a parent had a painful childhood, and his or her child has an easier life or is excelling in areas in which he or she did not excel. A common example is a pretty teenage daughter who had a great relationship with her mother. Then as she gets into high school, she becomes a cheerleader, she is very popular, and the guys like her. Pretty soon she is pulling away from Mom, picking up many new friends, which is entirely normal. But Mom begins to get jealous and resentful, and soon that resentment becomes full blown envy.

Another common example is a dad whose son is getting big; he's a football player, and feeling pretty cocky about himself, a typical teenager. Excitedly, he reports to his father, "I bench pressed 150 pounds today, Dad!" Dad callously reacts, "So what. At your age, I was doing more." Amazingly, we behave like that when we envy our kids. We must guard our hearts against these things.

Are you blessing and encouraging your children in all their gifts and talents? Are you excited about them? Are you cheering them on? Are you talking about their talents often, or are you only pointing out the negatives, the bad things? We need to recognize the gifts our kids have and exhort them often.

> *But the wisdom that is from above is first pure, then peaceable, gentle, willing to yield, full of mercy and good fruits, without partiality and without hypocrisy. Now the fruit of righteousness is sown in peace by those who make peace.*
>
> —James 3:17-18

Don't Be a Windbag

Love does not parade itself or brag, saying things like, "You know, when I was your age I had it much harder than you. I didn't even have a dad!"

Or, "My dad used to beat me with a belt."

"I never got a ride to school. I had to walk both ways, uphill, in the snow."

"I had to do all the chores."

These types of statements often attach them-selves to our disciplining. But this is not discipline, it is bragging. A synonym for the word brag is "windbag[2]." Is that what we should be striving for? Of course not. Bragging does not discipline. Do we honestly think our teenagers can relate to our child-hood? They cannot. So do not brag; it is wrong.

Truthfully, it is hard not to pull this card when our children are complaining and whining. "Ohhhh, I've got to walk to school"—when they have just one block to walk. Kids are lazy; this has not changed. Socrates made a statement around 400 BC that says in part, *"Children today are tyrants. They contradict their parents, gobble their food, and tyrannize their teachers[3]."* No matter how hard it is, however, we must choose not to brag, but to encourage them.

"Let another man praise you, and not your own mouth; a stranger, and not your own lips" (Prov. 27:2). We do not ever need to impress our children with how great and wise we are, nor belittle them in order to show them how important we are, saying things like, "I never talked to my parents that way when I was your age," and so on and so forth. *"For not he who commends himself is approved, but whom the Lord commends"* (2 Cor. 10:18).

Be a Team Player—Not a Dictator

Love is not puffed up or arrogant. We are not to be dictators ruling or lording over our children brutally or with fear and arrogance. God wants us to train up our children, not control them. Our atti-tude must reflect that we are for them in every situation, helping them mature as God wants them to be. Our children should feel like they are part of a team working together in this journey of raising them, not soldiers in an army.

Some parents, mainly men, miss this point, especially those of you who have been in the military or raised in a military family. Some parents tend to think they need to trap their children instead of train them. We tell our kids, "I know you're lying. I'm going to catch you." Then they plot and plan how they can catch their children in the act of foolishness.

I often hear teenagers saying, "I think my parents are always trying to catch me." That is not a team working together, but more like an enemy hoping to win against you. Can you imagine a quarterback saying to a lineman, "I'm watching you," or the lineman to the quarterback, "You'd better throw the ball to the guy I want, or I'm going to let this defender cream you"? What kind of team is that?

". . . Nor as being lords over those entrusted to you, but being examples to the flock" (1 Pet. 5:3). In other words, we should not aim at being a dictator with the flock God has committed to our charge. We must be concerned that we exemplify Him, not become some tyrant. *"An arrogant man stirs up strife, but he who trusts in the LORD will prosper"* (Prov. 28:25 NASB).

How Rude!

Love does not behave rudely or act unbecomingly, as in embarrassing and/or demeaning our child by discussing his or her failures or shortcomings with others, or by angrily spanking him, or spanking him or her in front of other people, including their siblings. Many parents seem to think that they can expose their children's sinful behavior without even considering whether their other kids are listening or not. Moms, not to pick on you, but a common sinful practice happens when you get on the phone with your friends . . . "Oh you won't believe the day I had. First my son did this, then he did that, then he did this," all the while your child is in the other room listening as you expose his sins and failures to whomever. *"Let no corrupt word proceed out of your mouth, but what is good for necessary edification, that it may impart grace to the hearers"* (Eph. 4:29). Even at church, I often hear people going on and on about their child's mistakes while he is sitting right there. Yes, there is a time and place for us to seek counsel, but we must never expose their sinful behaviors to anyone. Never!

Our children know our faults, don't they? They have seen and heard things that you and I have done wrong at home. Could you imagine if one Sunday morning at church the teachers that were watching your beautiful little children said to them, "We're going to have prayer time, so anyone who wants to come up and pray, come on up." So your little eight-year-old boy goes up and says, "Lord, I pray for my mom and dad. They yell, they argue, they scream, and they use bad language." How would you feel if you heard that had happened? You would be so embarrassed, you would probably quit going to that church! We would not want our children to expose us like that; it stands to reason they do not want us to do it either.

Adapt—Don't Compromise

Love does not seek to have its own way. In other words, we cannot insist that our children do only what we want them to do and not do. For example, I had a couple in my office. Right from the start, it was obvious that the mother was wearing the pants in the family as far as what the kids did and did not do. She sat in my office venting about how angry she was with her fourteen-year-old son. In the process of her venting, she came across the subject of paintball. "My son wants to play paintball. Paintball is so bad; I think it's so wrong."

I said, "Dad, what do you think about it?"

He replied, "Well, I think it's OK."

She jumped in, "Well, I think it is wrong. You shoot at people in paintball!"

I said to her, "Mom, I play paintball. I've shot my kids so many times! It's great fun, we love playing paintball. Your son is different from you, Mom, have you noticed?"

This same mom did not want her son to have a skateboard either, because "all skaters are bad, they wear their hats backwards and wear sagging pants." I explained to her "Mom, I know you don't like it, but it's not about you!" I said to the father, "If you think it's OK, you need to step up and lead; tell your wife you believe this is OK and that she needs to trust you in this and not treat her son with contempt because he is enjoying paintball."

Now . . . my wife would never play paintball with my kids and me; it is not her "thing" either. But since we boys enjoy it, she knows it is not up to her. When I take my shirt off after a game, and I have bruises on my body, she says, "You liked that? Didn't it hurt?"

"Oh yeah, it hurt bad. But yes, I liked it. I think it's great fun and so do the boys."

My son is a surfer. When he got his driver's license, he could not wait to drive to the beach and ride his surfboard. But my wife said, "Oh no, I think he should stay right here in our city for at least the next six months."

I replied, "Well, let's give him a couple of months. Eventually, after he has had some experience under his belt, I will let him drive me to the beach and see how he does. If he does fine, I will let him drive to the beach alone."

It is important to let your wife express her concerns and to involve her in these decisions and to try and work with her concerns and come up with a plan or solution, but the final decision lies with the father in this situation.

We have to be careful not to let our selfish opinions, fears, or what we like and dislike dictate what we allow our kids to do. Our kids are different than we are. We need to allow them to experiment in things, within the context of both morality and safety, obviously.

I have heard parents say, "Well, I don't let them listen to that 'rock junk.' I know it's Christian, but it has an evil beat." Is there really such a thing as an evil beat? There are even people who put on conferences regarding the "evil of rock music"; people pay to go see them. I challenge you to find that in the Bible! There is no such thing as an evil beat. There are evil lyrics and evil actions, but there is no evil beat. My point is that there is a wide variety of music that kids like that may be very different from our taste. If it is Christian and the lyrics are OK, fine—what is the problem?—let them listen.

We should not be inflexible or too rigid, constantly controlling the things we allow our kids to do for the wrong reasons. Instead, we should always try and cooperate or help them enjoy their interests. But never compromising our faith or what the Bible stands for.

We need to *pursue* our kids and their different interests. My son Nicholas loves surfing. During his adolescence, I remember so many times going out with him in the winter time, fifty-four degrees water, six-foot waves. On many occasions, just getting out past the waves nearly killed me. I was freezing half the time and exhausted, but praise the Lord, I was out there with my boy having fun. On some of these surf outings, I would rather have been doing something else, but he asked me to join him. So we went.

Each child is different. My daughter likes to jump on the trampoline or take our dog for a walk . . . not so much fun for me, but I do it.

Just to give an example of how important it is to do things with your kids, when my daughter was ten years old, she wrote me a Father's Day card. This is how she described why she loved her daddy:

These are the reasons I love you, Daddy

Number one, you go on the trampoline with me. Number two, you take me to Dairy Queen. [OK, I like that one—that's no sacrifice for me!] *Number three, you take my dog for walks with me. Number four, you play soccer with me. Number five, you take me on bike rides. Number six, you take me on a motor-cycle ride. Number seven, you read with me. Number eight, you make me breakfast. Number nine, you play cards with me.*

Notice that every reason my daughter listed was an *action*. It was me giving her time. It was not insincere words, "Oh, Honey, I love you. Here's a hug. See you later." Love is all about actions and time spent. Every one of our kids needs it; we need to remember and practice this on a continuous basis.

The best defense in keeping our kids from pulling away from us too soon is a strong offense of spending time with them, both individually and as a family, but also showing proper affection towards them. Many times I have heard dads tell me, "Well, I'm not a hugger."

I love telling them, "Well, it's not about *you*. I don't care if you're a hugger. You have a child who loves and needs to be hugged. Do something about it."

Dads, we may tell ourselves that Mom has been making up for our lack, but it does not work that way. We need to get rid of whatever fear we have and say, "I am going to become a hugger." Then ask God to change your heart to make you a hugger for your hugger kid.

My older son, Nicholas, is not a big hugger. He never was. His way of receiving affection was to jump on my back and wrestle with me. So we wrestled. My son Justin, even at seventeen-years old, standing three inches taller than me now, would still lay on my lap, pleading, "Scratch my back." There were many nights during Justin's adolescence and up to nineteen years of age, when we would say our prayers, he would lay right next to me, and I would rub his head, scratch his back or rub his feet. He loves being touched.

Each kid is different, and it is important to treat them that way. Most parents who struggle with showing affection never pray about it. They never ask God to change them or examine themselves to see why they find it so difficult. If that is you—stop right now and ask God to help you in this area.

We must remember that it is not about us; if our child needs affection, and we feel uncomfortable, we need to say, "God, change me." It is not our will, but God's will. We need to glorify Him, even when we have a hard time showing affection to our kids.

Often past issues are the cause of difficulty in showing or giving affection: those who had parents who failed them, or who did not show affection. If they are harboring bitterness toward that parent and have not forgiven them, if they have not trusted the Lord with their past, this issue becomes a "grace clogger" in their lives.

God wants to pour transforming power into our lives to change us into the affectionate parents

He wants us to be for the children He brought into our lives. But if we have not trusted the Lord and forgiven our parents, this can be the reason you are unable to receive that transforming power. This is a very common problem. We must die to our flesh and love our children however they need to receive it.

"Let no one seek his own, but each one the other's well-being" (1 Cor. 10:24).

"For you, brethren, have been called to liberty; only do not use liberty as an opportunity for the flesh, but through love serve one another" (Gal. 5:13).

Don't Keep Score

Love thinks no evil. We cannot keep score of our children's failures in order to beat them over the head with them later. Sadly, this is a common method many parents use during discipline. Our child makes a mistake, we have a little discussion. But then rather than letting it go, we place the incident in our "back pocket." Then Friday night comes up and our son says, "Hey, can I go out tonight?"

"No! Remember what you did last Tuesday? Sorry. You aren't going anywhere." This method of discipline is so damaging and wrong. It is the opposite of love; love keeps no record of wrongs.

Discipline needs to happen immediately, and then we move on—we cannot hold onto it. Feelings are good passengers, but poor drivers. We must let truth, not our feelings, dictate how we react and respond to our children, even when it comes to disciplining them.

Pursue peace with all people, and holiness, without which no one will see the Lord: looking carefully lest anyone fall short of the grace of God; lest any root of bitterness springing up cause trouble, and by this many become defiled.

— Hebrews 12:14-15

"Become defiled" means that because we have harbored bitterness about something our child has done, we begin to spill poison out infecting and hurting those around us. Sadly, many times we have had thoughts of evil towards our children when we meditate upon their failures, harboring bitterness; or ignore them, pout, stay angry for days. These practices are the opposite of love. Many parents never consider the fact that they are practicing the opposite of love. We must choose not to think evil.

The NIV version of 1 Corinthians 13:5 says love *"keeps no record of wrongs."* The New King James Version says love *"thinks no evil."* But I especially like the way The Living Bible says it: love *"is not irritable or touchy. It does not hold grudges, and will hardly even notice when others do it wrong."* That is the real meaning of 1 Corinthians 13:5, and that is how we must behave.

Unforgiveness is a poison that one takes, hoping to kill the other person. Truly, unforgiveness is like a cancer. If we allow it to, it will devour us from the inside and infect everyone around us in a negative way.

As a parent, we have the opportunity to forgive our children daily. Many parents have the wrong perspective when it comes to their children breaking a rule or disobeying. God does not want us to take it personally, but to see and perceive every foolish act or failure our children make as an opportunity to train them, not taking it personally and becoming angry or hurt.

When someone wrongs us, God says, *"You ought rather to forgive and comfort him, lest perhaps such a one be swallowed up with too much sorrow. Therefore I urge you to reaffirm your love to him"* (2 Cor. 2:7-8).

How often should we forgive? Always—seventy times seven. God's Word is clear on this.

"And be kind to one another, tenderhearted, forgiving one another, even as God in Christ forgave you" (Eph. 4:32).

Are You Mocking Me?

Love does not rejoice in iniquity. Have you ever said to your child, "I told you so! You deserve what you got. I told you that you would get in trouble. I was right"? When our child makes a mistake, we should never act like we are happy that they got caught or got into trouble or got hurt. God does not want us to react in the flesh; He wants us to respond in love, even when they deliberately do some foolish thing.

Proverbs 14:9 says, *"Fools mock at sin, but among the upright there is favor."* There were times when in my heart I was happy that Nick got what he deserved, but I did not show it. We need to exercise self-control. Proverbs 24:17 says, *"Do not rejoice when your enemy falls, and do not let your heart be glad when he stumbles."*

The Truth Is . . .

Love rejoices in the truth. When we fail to praise our children and instead constantly point out their faults, we are not rejoicing in the truth. One of the questions we ask parents when they come in for counseling is: "If your teenager was here and I asked him, on an average day, how much of your conversation or communication with him is positive versus negative, what would he say?"

Positive communication is, "How are you doing? You look nice. What happened at school today?" Negative is, "Stop that, leave your sister alone! Do your homework! Take out the trash!"

Quite often parents respond, "Oh, that's an easy one. It's 90 percent negative. Every day." Days turn into weeks, and weeks turn into months, all the while we are poisoning our kids, sinning against them, not loving them, because we are consumed with pointing out what they are not doing and not thinking about praising them.

Instead, we need to be actively pursuing the good things in our kids. I know it is hard with those strong-willed kids. I remember telling Nick many times, "You're strong-willed, that's good." That's all I could come up with! There were days I had to pray to come up with something good to say.

If this has been happening in your family, turn it around. At night when you have your family prayer time, take a moment and say, "OK everyone, say something good about each other." Make it a fun thing. Get the whole family started on looking for the good things in each other. It is so important that we work together as a team; Dad or Mom—you start it off.

Personally, sometimes I have a tendency to micro-manage. The minute I walk into the house, I begin to notice what's out of place or everyone's faults. "Who left that on the floor?"

True, the faults need to be fixed, but we must fix them with loving discipline and training. But making sure we are keeping ourselves in check in this area is so important.

My wife has been such a blessing to me in this area. She encouraged me to walk into the house and relax without saying a word about what is out of place or what didn't get done; to let the kids come and talk to me for thirty to forty minutes before I begin pointing out what needs to be done.

There are ways we can rejoice in our children other than just verbal. My wife was putting away some clothes in my older son's drawer and found every letter that I had ever written to him. Praise God they were good letters! I did not say, "You little brat . . ." Instead, the letters were filled with, "I love you. You're making me so proud. I am so happy to see your gifts and your talent in music." My wife and I cried as we read through them. He had saved every one, and so had my son Justin. God has given us such influential power as dads and as moms! We need to use that power to bless and praise them.

"Let love be without hypocrisy. Abhor what is evil. Cling to what is good" (Rom. 12:9).

"I have no greater joy than to hear that my children walk in truth" (3 John 4).

Grin and Bear It

Love bears all things, meaning we avoid criticizing or neglecting our children because they failed to meet our expectations. *"Bear one another's burdens, and so fulfill the law of Christ"* (Gal. 6:2). "To bear" means to endure and suffer patiently[4]. Love does not give up, or tell our kids that "we just can't take it anymore!" and then let the house run amuck. We cannot do that. We need to be faithful to support our children in all seasons of life. We should not play "head games" and treat them with contempt. We must remain in our jobs as ministers, continuously patient, disciplining them properly in love.

My son Justin never seemed to mind spending hours doing homework. Neither my wife nor I could relate to that; we both disliked homework. Nick, on the other hand, hated homework and tried to avoid it like the plague. From the time Nick hit junior high all the way through the end of high school, if we did not sit down with him while he did his homework, he would never, ever have done it. So every night my wife and I shared this often unpleasant homework time with Nick; one of us would either finish the dinner or do the dishes while the other sat down and did homework with Nick.

I had a single mother come into my office complaining about the same situation. "Every night when I come home from work, I'm so tired, but if I don't sit down with my son, he just dillydallies and takes one hour's worth of homework and makes it three hours. Every night I'm yelling and screaming at him and he won't change. It is ridiculous. I've never had to sit down with my older son; he comes home and just does it. I'm so upset, what do I do to fix it?"

I calmly replied, "Sit down and do his homework with him."

"But aren't I supposed to train him?"

"Yes, but right now he needs you. His actions are saying, 'Mom, I need you to sit down with me, I need your help, I need your structure in this area.'" I told her, "You can't compare him to your older son. Instead, remind yourself every night 'this is my time with my son' and do his homework with him. What else are you doing that is more important?" The poor woman had spent the first eight years of this kid's life comparing him to his brother and being angry every night, instead of just sitting down and doing the homework with him.

We must bear with our kids. Children who struggle academically and/or are strong-willed take more time and energy. The question for us parents is, "Do you accept the child God gave you and the ministry He has put before you to do?" He will give you the strength to do it if you ask Him and quit complaining.

Believe It or Not

Love believes all things. We need to have a willingness to always pursue a trusting relationship, even when there has been dishonesty. Too often I see parents doubting what their child says before they know the facts. Many times they say, "My kid's a liar. I can put up with anything, but when they lie, ohhh."

I actually love it when parents say that, because I look right at them and reply, "You're a liar! You lie all the time; you lie to God every day. Why would you put an expectation upon your kid that you don't have on yourself?"

They are inflamed: "What do you mean?"

"Do you love God with all your heart, mind, body and soul?"

"Of course I do."

"Did you tell Him that today?"

"Oh, uh, well . . ."

"You say you love God, but how many minutes did you spend with Him today?"

"Um . . ."

The perspective that lying is "the mother of all bad things to do" can exasperate our children and provoke them to continue that behavior. We lie to God all the time, so we cannot elevate lying above all other sins. Instead, we must simply unemotionally discipline them. You can have a rule that states, "If you lie, the consequences are double."

I have found that in cases where kids are constantly lying, the parents are the ones that have to change first. We must quit getting angry, being judgmental; saying things like, "I don't trust you" or "I know I'm going to catch you." Love hopes all things-not doubts all things.

"Now hope does not disappoint, because the love of God has been poured out in our hearts by the Holy Spirit who was given to us" (Rom. 5:5).

Go the Extra Mile

Love endures all things. To "endure" means to outlast, to tolerate[5]. True, it is hard work being a parent. But we must ask ourselves, does our difficult child know through our daily actions toward him/her that we accept them, that we are willing to love them and adjust to their strong will? Do they know that we are willing to give the extra 10 or 20 percent, or 100 percent, that it takes? Or does he believe "Mom and Dad don't like me or like me less than my brother/sister"?

Does a five-year-old strong-willed child know why he thinks the way he does? Of course not. Do you think he understands why, when we say, "Don't cross that line," the first thing that crosses his mind is, "You don't think I am able to so I must show you I can"? No, our kids do not know why they are wired the way they are. When we are constantly getting angry rather than enduring, the message to our children is "You love them less." Period. That is their perception.

Instead, we have got to say, "OK, God, You brought me this mule. I've got to accept this and endure this in Your power and might, not mine." Remember your transformation. What has the Lord been revealing in you through this child?

Do What Comes Unnaturally

Much of our problem in loving our children is that we do not understand how to discipline properly and how to view the mistakes and foolishness that comes out of our children. Once we master those tools and learn how to work together as a team, however, our and their frustrations will be alleviated.

"Fathers, do not provoke your children, lest they become discouraged" (Col. 3:21).

"A soft answer turns away wrath, but a harsh word stirs up anger" (Prov. 15:1).

Love never fails. When someone mistreats us, as parent ministers God wants us to do what comes supernaturally, not naturally. Naturally, when someone does not live up to our expectations, we want to react in our flesh. But God says, "No, as My ministers, I want you to respond in a supernatural way," just as Christ has responded to us.

Let no corrupt word proceed out of your mouth, but what is good for necessary edification, that it may impart grace to the hearers. And do not grieve the Holy Spirit of God, by whom you were sealed for the day of redemption. Let all bitterness, wrath, anger, clamor, and evil speaking be put away from you, with all malice. And be kind to one another, tenderhearted, forgiving one another, even as God in Christ forgave you.

—Ephesians 4:29-32

This passage encapsulates the kind of love that God has called us to as parent ministers. Remember, if God gave us a command that He could not enable us to fulfill, that would make Him a liar. But He does not lie.

God does not want to make us feel condemned. Rather, He wants us to pray, to seek Him for the power to love our children the way we should. He tells us, "Whatever you ask in My name, I will give you" (John 16:23).

It is true that God chose us to be parents knowing how foolish and selfish we were. But He did not do it with the idea that we would stay that way. He expects us to dig into His Word and to build and maintain a foundation that will allow that Word to bring transformation in our hearts. He has told us, "I will give you the ability, through the power of the Holy Spirit, through your intimate relationship with Me, to accomplish every single command" (Phil. 4:13 paraphrased).

Praise God!

---

[1] http:www.cdc.gov/ncbddd/adhd/symptom.htm

[2] Thesaurus.com

[3] William L. Patty and Louise S. Johnson, *Personality and Adjustment,* p. 277 (1953)

[4] *Webster's II New Riverside Dictionary Revised Edition, Office Edition*, Houghton Mifflin Company, 1996

[5] *Webster's II New Riverside Dictionary Revised Edition, Office Edition*, Houghton Mifflin Company, 1996

CHAPTER SIX

Healthy Communication

Communication, or the act of communicating, is the exchange of thought, message, or information[1]. It is possible to communicate without saying a word; however, real communication requires listening. God had more in mind when He gave us two ears than just balancing out the way our head looks. We have two ears and one mouth for a good reason.

Listening involves paying close attention. It is a very common practice that, when our kids want to talk to us, we just keep doing what we are doing without really listening, and we think they are not aware or unaffected by this. But true loving communication requires that we really listen and be in tune. Since situations requiring a parent to take some disciplinary action often contain a lot of emotions on the part of the parent and child, let's look at the impact of the different elements involved in communication during such emotional times.

What They See

Our facial expression, what our kids see on our face, is 55 percent of our communication[2]. We must be very mindful of this whenever we are communicating to our children.

Let me give you an example: you are driving home one night with your children in the back seat, and somebody cuts in front of you, nearly causing you to swerve off the road. You react in frustration: "Oh, you stupid . . . blank, blank, blank," and your face reflects the anger you feel. Then you arrive home and your kids are buzzing from all the cookies and candy they have had, and they do not want to get in bed. You tell them once, "Go to bed," and they will not do it, so you put on the exact same face that you put on toward the guy who cut you off and yell at them, "I told you to get in your bed right now!" Your children's perception at that moment is that you see them or value them the same way you did that stranger who nearly ran you off the road . . . Ouch! Our facial expressions can be sinful and unloving.

What They Hear

Our tone of voice comprises 38 percent of our communication[3]. Every time we raise our voice or yell at our children, we are communicating our anger through more than just our words. Think about this: if we add together facial expressions and tone of voice, 55 percent and 38 percent, we get 93 percent! So when we are twisting our faces with anger, resentment, or disappointment and elevating our voices, we are communicating 93 percent negatively. Why do we think we have to do this during or make it a part of discipline, in order for it to work? Where did that come from? Let me tell you where it comes from: it comes from the pit of hell. Our flesh and the devil have used this type of communication from parents to destroy many a life.

Surprisingly, verbal communication accounts for only 7 percent of all communication[4]. We need to remind ourselves that what is actually falling out of our mouth is only 7 percent of communication. So those of you who think you have to lecture, if only 7 percent of what you are saying is being heard, why waste your breath? After two minutes of lecturing, when we are disciplining our children, all our children hear is blah, blah, blah, blah, blah. Our facial expressions are a huge part of what we communicate: the stare, the glare, etc. We need to watch what "we say" with our faces.

So many teens tell me, "My parents don't love me, and they don't care." They believe this because their parents are communicating negatively or sinfully on an ongoing basis. It is no wonder that so many kids are struggling with self-worth. A child's self-worth comes from how their parents show that they love, care for, and value them. When you and I misrepresent God on a daily basis, we create what I call the EDTNI syndrome: emotionally deprived through negative input. So many kids are struggling with this. Those kids who are affected by this are more prone to all types of addiction or emotional problems: drugs, pornography, alcohol, and unhealthy relationships are only a few. Then many of them become parents and pass it on.

It Starts With the Heart

- Loving communication begins with the heart.

"But those things which proceed out of the mouth come from the heart, and they defile a man" (Matt. 15:18).

"A good man out of the good treasure of his heart brings forth good things, and an evil man out of the evil treasure brings forth evil things" (Matt. 12:35).

"Good treasure" goes back to our strong foundation. If you or I are putting the Word of God in our hearts, guess what is going to come out? Good things.

- Loving communication is based upon the value we have placed on another person.

Love involves being Christ-centered, not self-centered. It is the decision to place value on a person. *"Behold, children are a gift of the Lord"* (Ps. 127:3 NASB). This means our toddlers are a gift, and so are our teens.

Let me give you an example of valuing others. If you invited your pastor over for dinner, would you find out what his favorite dish is before he came? Would you make sure your house is clean? Would you be very careful not to say the wrong thing so you didn't offend him? Would you make sure that your kids were going to behave? How would you dress?

Of course you would put your best foot forward. Why? Because you value your pastor. I am sure your pastor is a good guy, and is worth valuing—but not more than your children.

Our kids are not dumb; they see us devalue them every day. Sadly, we do not even consider our actions. This is not OK. Valuing someone is a choice, and God's Word says this child is a gift from God. He has placed high value upon our kids, and we must choose always to treat them that way and take responsibility when we don't by asking for forgiveness.

- Loving communication is a learned skill.

Being Christ-centered not self-centered is a choice. We need to learn how to do it. So many of us know that we need to change some sinful way in our communication with our children, but yet do nothing about it. It is God's will that we communicate love, and since that is the case, if we pray about changing so that we may exemplify and glorify Him, He will bring about that change in our hearts.

"The heart of the righteous studies how to answer, but the mouth of the wicked pours forth evil" (Prov. 15:28).

"From a wise mind comes wise speech; the words of the wise are persuasive" (Prov. 16:23 NLT).

In order to accomplish this change, we must begin to look at our children through a whole different set of lenses. God wants us to see our children through His eyes and through what His Word says. I love this statement from Warren Wiersbe: "Ministry takes place when divine resources meet human needs through loving channels to the glory of God[5]." That divine resource is that abiding relationship in Christ, our foundation.

Dedication and Training

"Train up a child in the way he should go, and when he is old he will not depart from it" (Prov. 22:6). Many people think this passage offers some type of guarantee, that if we do everything perfect, our children will come out OK. But it does not work that way. You can be the best parent you can be, and your kid could still turn out to be a maniac living an immoral life. Why? Because God gave them free choice, just like He gave us.

There is no guarantee that, if we do everything right, our children will turn out right. That is not what God's Word says here. The word "train" in the original Hebrew is *chanak,* which means "to dedicate or set aside for divine service." In other words, we need to be mindful at all times that our children are not our own, but the Lord's, and we need to treat them that way—always. We must dedicate them back unto the Lord.

When we bring our babies up front on Sunday mornings to dedicate them, it is an important event. We stand before the entire congregation, saying to ourselves as parents, and to the congregation, "We are publicly dedicating this child back unto You, Lord. He/she is not mine, they are Yours. This child is Yours, God, and I want to believe that and treat them that way as long as they are in my care."

That is what God is saying in this passage found in Proverbs 22:6: dedicate your children unto the Lord, and remember they are not yours.

We will not be held responsible for the choices our children make, but for the choices we make in raising them. We are often so concerned about the mistakes our kids are going to make, and how they will embarrass us, that it dictates the way we love them—or should I say, do not love them. We must understand that the value of our children comes from what God has said, not their personalities, failures, or their stage of life. God said, "This is My gift to you."

Many times I felt like wrapping Nick up and sending him back. "God, I don't want this one. He is too much work." But I didn't have a choice in the matter, did I? Neither do you. God knew exactly what we needed.

Does this change if you are a single parent, blended family, foster parent, or grandparent raising kids? No, it does not.

Let's pause for a reality check. Did you know that your children are gifts from God? Do you always treat them that way? That is our battleground. It is as if God said, "Here's My gift to you, and here are some clear instructions on how I want you to treat it. Follow my directions, I'll be checking up on you." Should we try our best and desire to do what God says? Absolutely!

The manual that God gave us to guide us on how to treat our children is the Word of God. And the manual says, "Love them; treat them as a gift *always.*"

Their Unique Personalities

The second part of Proverbs 22:6 says, *". . . in the way he should go."* "The way he should go" is a Hebrew idiom that literally means, "upon the mouth of his ways," or according to the demands of his or her personality, conduct, stage of life, or natural bent. What this means is that we are to treat each one of our kids as a gift no matter how they act or what their individual personalities are. God wants us to adapt to the personalities He has given them.

Beginning with the first family, we see evidence of these different personalities. Cain was self-willed and determined to go his own way—a strong-willed mule. Abel, on the other hand, who loved the Lord, was a sensitive and more compliant child.

Jacob and Esau were twins—same mom, same dad. But Jacob was a momma's boy, smooth skinned, always in the kitchen; while Esau was a man's man, rough, a hunter, a really gruff guy. Twins, yet different personalities, different people. God has been doing this from the beginning of time.

It is funny how parents who received a strong-willed child often act like we got the short end of the stick with our particular kids, but we did not. God knew what He was doing, and He does not make mistakes. Do you believe that?

". . . As the LORD lives, who made our very souls . . ." (Jer. 38:16). God is the creator of the soul, which is the mind, will, and emotion. You and I had something to do with the color of our child's eyes, hair, their size, and the color of their skin, but when it comes to their mind, will, and emotions, we

had nothing to do with it. Yes, they will pick up our traits, but their mind, will, and emotions were given by God, and He did not make a mistake.

We must quit blaming our spouse, our parents, and our step-parents. Instead, blame God for the bent that your child has, for his/her personality, because God is the one who made them the way they are. Psalm 139:13 says, *"For You formed my inward parts; You covered me in my mother's womb."*

God made our souls; He breathed life into us. He formed us in our mother's womb, and our kids also. The Word says that *all* of us are fearfully and wonderfully made. When we get angry and resentful at our kids and begin to misrepresent Christ, we are acting like He made a mistake. Colossians 3:21 says, *"Fathers, do not provoke your children, lest they become discouraged."* Yet many parents provoke their children by not practicing biblical love and not considering their children a gift of God.

There is a time and season for all things, Ecclesiastes 3:1 tells us, which includes the "terrible twos" and even the difficult season of adolescence. God designed these seasons. It was not a mistake. Proverbs 22:6 is not a guarantee, but it is clear instruction regarding how we need to become students of our children, adapting to their personalities and being willing to accept the fact that one may need more instruction, discipline, and time than another. Some are going to take a lot more energy. When we follow the will of God in our parenting, we are not provided a guarantee, but we are released from guilt.

We must always remember the influential power God has given us over our kids. No one has more power and influence over our kids than we do, especially us dads. Our influence is like no one else's. We must always remember that.

Our children's minds are like tape recorders, and for the first twelve or thirteen years they are on "record." But when they hit adolescence, they switch to playback. At that point, we are often just reaping what we sowed over and over from the years previous.

If we truly love God and want to please Him, and if our desire is to serve Him, we will pay no attention to the distinctions made by natural individuality, personalities, failures, or stages of life our children are going through. If our desire is to please the Lord and do it His way, then when they are revealing their natural bent and personality, we will not let that dictate how we are responding or reacting to them. As a minister for the Lord, we have no business being guided by our natural temperament, but by His Word and the Holy Spirit.

Nick has been a strong-willed child from the day he was born. I still remember watching my wife deliver him. The pregnancy and even the delivery were so hard, it was scary. He would not come out for hours. He was even stubborn about being born! I could just imagine him in there crying, "No, I'm not coming out!" holding on to my wife's insides.

My wife struggled for almost nine hours, then finally the doctor picked up some scary-looking forceps; I immediately began getting queasy.

He started to pull really hard, all the while I was thinking, "Hey Doc, you're going to pull his head off!" Suddenly I heard, "Pop!" and there was Nick's head. There was no spanking needed; he came out screaming, telling everybody right from the start, "I'm in control and I am angry at you all."

I cut his umbilical cord, then the nurse walked him over to the scale; and, I will never forget this, as she put him on the scale, he put his arms out and arched his back and almost flipped over. The nurse cried, "Oh my gosh!" and jumped back. That was the first sign we were in trouble! And Nick has been that way since day one, stubborn and strong-willed.

At three years old, he had never taken a nap in his life. Unless he had a 103° temperature, he did not sleep. The minute the sun was up, he was up. He had more energy than any human being I knew. He was just bent and determined, "I'm gonna rule and do what I want when I want." That is the way God wired him.

Every kid is different, and each one needs our love.

---

[1] *Webster's II New Riverside Dictionary Revised Edition, Office Edition*, Houghton Mifflin Company, 1996

[2] See Albert Mehrabian's Rule

[3] See Albert Mehrabian's Rule

[4] See Albert Mehrabian's Rule

[5] *On Being a Servant of God*, by Warren Wiersbe; Thomas Nelson Publishers, 1993

CHAPTER SEVEN

The Main Reasons We Fail to Love

Unforgiveness

There are four main reasons we fail in the way that we love our children. The most common reason is un-forgiveness we carry from our pasts. As I explained in a previous chapter, if we are harboring bitterness towards our parents, an ex-spouse, our children, our current spouse, whomever, that un-forgiveness prevents us from completing the transformation that God desires for us.

"Therefore, if anyone is in Christ, he is a new creation; old things have passed away; behold, all things have become new" (2 Cor. 5:17).

Many of us who come to Christ have experienced terrible situations in our pasts: divorce, abandonment, rejection, and mistreatment. We say we have forgiven those people who hurt us; we even tell God we have forgiven them. But we treat the act of forgiveness as if it is merely an escape clause to excuse our hurts and pains. In reality, our natural self-defense mechanism is to stuff the pain of our past, to ignore the situation and act like it never happened. But we really have not followed God's instruction in how to forgive.

Many Christians today, when they hit adolescence, were hurting because of the lack of love and affection in their childhood; this creates a void, which many tried to fill with drugs, pornography, unhealthy relationships, anorexia, bulimia, overeating, and the many other things that the enemy provides as counterfeit "antidotes" to take the pain away. Unfortunately, most of the people who tried to help them out of their situations dealt only with their behavior, not the motives behind it. Then they became Christians and realized how bad that behavior was, so they stopped. Yet they still never dealt with the reasons they started in the first place. And now they cannot figure out why they are repeating in their own families the same sinful behaviors their parents did to them.

If we find ourselves stuck in a rut, unable to grow in Christ, or repeating sinful, unloving habits that our parents did to us, one of the things we must do as Christians is examine ourselves and ask the Lord if there is something that we haven't dealt with in our past. This is not to blame anyone for our behavior, but to find understanding.

Thankfully, there is an antidote for the past hurts or un-forgiveness found in God's Word: *"For if you forgive men their trespasses, your heavenly Father will also forgive you. But if you do not forgive men their trespasses, neither will your Father forgive*

your trespasses" (Matt. 6:14-15). This is not a salvation issue; it is a grace, healing, transformation issue.
Colossians 3:13 says, *"bearing with one another,
and forgiving one another, if anyone has a complaint
against another; even as Christ forgave you, so you
also must do."*

Often, when we hear the word "forgiveness," we
attach all kinds of requirements to it in our minds.
But when God said "forgiveness," He did not say
that the offender will agree with you. He did not say
that the offender will ask you to forgive them. He did
not say that the offender will accept your forgiveness and/or agree with you about whether what they
did was wrong or bad. And He did not say that the
relationship has to be restored. He just said that we
must forgive.

If someone has hurt you and you have been
running from it, you need to deal with it biblically.
You can do it in a letter, on the telephone, via email,
or you can do it in person. Even if that person is dead,
you can sit down with a witness—your husband,
your wife, a brother in the Lord, and say, "I've
been harboring bitterness towards my dad, mom, or
whomever. So right now, God, I'm forgiving them.
They failed me, I know, but I'm trusting You right
now, God, to heal me. Please take this bitterness out
of my heart. Give me the strength to trust you, Lord,
that you didn't make a mistake when you made them
my dad or mom."

Harboring un-forgiveness could be one of the
main reasons why you are not growing and the love
of God is not flowing out of you. Forgive and move

on. It is awfully hard to forgive. It is harder not to forgive. If we do not forgive, we deny what Jesus has done for us on the cross (see Matt. 6:14-15). Our experience of God's forgiveness is directly related to our ability to forgive. A readiness to forgive others is part of the indication that we have truly repented and received God's forgiveness. A broken heart towards God cannot be a hard heart towards others.

Pride and fear keep us from forgiveness and reconciliation. Refusing to give in or be broken, insisting on our rights, and defending ourselves are all indications that our selfish pride is ruling our life, rather than the Lord. If fears of "what-ifs" are consuming and controlling you, you need to pray for the faith to trust and obey God. Enemies are very expensive to keep. Matthew 18:21-35 warns that an unforgiving heart will put us in an emotional prison.

We Were Set Up!

Another reason we fail to love our children is called the set-up.

> *For the weapons of our warfare are not carnal but mighty in God for pulling down strongholds, casting down arguments and every high thing that exalts itself against the knowledge of God, bringing every thought into captivity to the obedience of Christ (2 Cor. 10:4-5).*

We need to remind ourselves constantly that we are in the midst of warfare, and our heart and mind are the battleground. We must weigh every thought that comes into our minds against God's Word. Satan hates us and hates our kids, and the last thing he wants us to do is represent Christ in front of our children. He wants us to be mean and harsh, and to take the influence that God has given us and use it for his evil will, because that is the greatest tool that he has to push our kids away from God.

When a Christian man or woman misrepresents Christ every day in his home and shows contempt towards his kids on a daily basis, he is acting as the greatest tool to push his kids right into the hands of Satan. Sadly, many Christians are doing just that.

Once when Nick was about fourteen years old, I went to pick him up from youth group. I was there a little bit early, and, as I was waiting in the car, another father walked up to me and said, "Did you hear what happened? The kids ditched youth group. They split. They're down at some girl's house playing basketball. When my son gets back, I'm gonna give him a piece of my mind."

He stomped back to his truck, and I sat there and began to fume, "What's Nick doing at some girl's house? That little jerk. Boy, when he gets in the car, I'm gonna give him a piece of my mind too. I'm going to make him work." These thoughts kept firing in my head; pretty soon my veins were popping out of my neck and I was grabbing the steering wheel, thinking, "I can't wait."

But suddenly the Holy Spirit said, "What are you doing, Craig? Where are all these thoughts coming from? From the pit of hell. Do you remember when you were his age? Did you even want to go to a youth group? As a matter of fact, remember when you were kicked out when you were fourteen and asked not to come back? And you never wanted to go back. Nick *wants* to come to youth group." Immediately, I knew the Lord was right. So I took the time to think it through from His perspective. I had some time to pray and talk with the Lord.

When Nick finally came walking up, I had calmed way down. As he got into the car, he asked if a couple of friends could have rides home as well. I told them to jump in. We were not even out of the parking lot yet, when Nick said, "Hey, Dad, you know, we didn't go tonight. We got here, and they told us that we were all going down to San Diego to watch some graduation at some school. They said if we didn't want to go, we could call our parents. We didn't want to go with them, so one girl said, 'Come down to my house and play basketball, it's a block down the street.' So that's where we went." Right off the bat, he told me what had happened.

I replied, "OK, Nick. Next time, I want you to call and ask, OK? We need to know where you are in case something happens. Get permission to do that next time."

He said, "OK, Dad."

I found out later that when they were all walking back from this girl's house, back to the church, they were talking amongst themselves about how they were going to lie to their parents about where they had been. And my son Nick said, "Why are you going to lie? Just tell them the truth. It's stupid to lie." One little girl was so impressed that she went home and told her mother. Her mother was so impressed that she called my wife to let us know what my son had said.

Can you imagine, after Nick had encouraged these kids to tell the truth, if I had been an idiot and just blasted him when he came to the car—right in front of the kids he had just told to be honest to their parents? That is how the enemy works. He sends fiery darts into our minds continuously, and if we are not prepared, we will just suck them right in and let them infect the way we treat our children.

There are three voices all of us hear: the Holy Spirit (which is the one we should always listen to), our own (which we should usually ignore), and Satan's (which we should always ignore). Satan does indeed have access to our psyche. He cannot read our minds, but he can fire those darts at us. You can bet he is at your house, firing those darts whenever possible.

"And the Lord said, 'Simon, Simon! Indeed, Satan has asked for you, that he may sift you as wheat'" (Luke 22:31).

Satan has access to our homes, parents, and he is firing those darts. We need to take our thoughts captive and be sure the only voice we listen to is the Holy Spirit's.

"For we do not wrestle against flesh and blood, but against principalities, against powers, against the rulers of the darkness of this age, against spiritual hosts of wickedness in the heavenly places" (Eph. 6:12). Are there any negative, sinful thoughts that you regularly harbor about any of your children?

If the thoughts are unloving, you already know they are not of God.

The Problem of Persecution

Another common reason that we fail to love our kids is persecution or opposition. Matthew 5:43-45 tells us how we are supposed to act towards our opposition:

> *You have heard that it was said, "You shall love your neighbor and hate your enemy." But I say to you, love your enemies, bless those who curse you, do good to those who hate you, pray for those who spitefully use you and persecute you, that you may be sons of your Father in Heaven.*

As a parent, as a minister, this is the way God wants us to respond to our kids.

> *For what credit is it if, when you are beaten for your faults, you take it patiently? But when you do good and suffer, if you take it patiently, this is commendable before God. For to this you were called, because Christ also suffered for us, leaving us an example, that you should follow His steps.*
> —1 Peter 2:20-21

Sometimes we feel like our kids are our enemies. We feel like they are deliberately going out of their way to irritate us. Even if they are, God tells us how to respond to them. We are stewards entrusted by God to carry His message and plan to our children by word and by deed (our actions). We must examine our hearts daily and check our motives behind all that we do. Parenting can include suffering; at times, it is difficult, but the Word tells us: *"For it is better, if it is the will of God, to suffer for doing good than for doing evil"* (1 Pet. 3:17).

Who Me, Selfish?

Another common reason we fail to love is selfishness. Again, 1 Corinthians 13:5 tells us that love *"does not seek its own."*

"For all the law is fulfilled in one word, even in this: 'You shall love your neighbor as yourself'" (Gal. 5:14).

"Then He said to them all, 'If anyone desires to come after Me, let him deny himself, and take up his cross daily, and follow Me'" (Luke 9:23).

We do not realize how selfish and conditional we are until our children come home from the hospital and we begin to raise them. If they do not live up to our expectations, what do we do? "Oh, that's it; you crossed the line now, Buddy."

But God tells us we must not put selfish expectations upon our kids. Even though our children do not want to listen and they do not want to be trained, we need to train them faithfully without our anger and selfishness dictating how we respond to them. Perhaps your first child was a wonderful, easy, pleasing kid. Then the next one you believe is a Tasmanian Devil, and you spend so much time comparing the two.

"Why can't you just be like your sister?" Remember, one will never be the same as the other. We cannot put selfish demands upon our kids. What is the Lord revealing in you that is selfish?

Scripture tells us that God tests us; He examines our hearts and shows us how conditional and selfish we are. *"But as we have been approved by God to be entrusted with the Gospel, even so we speak, not as pleasing men, but God who tests our hearts"* (1 Thess. 2:4).

In order for metal to be purified, it must be placed in huge vats with extensive heat underneath. As the metal inside becomes red hot, all kinds of black stuff, called *dross,* begins coming to the surface. The dross is the impurity inside the metal, which is scooped off the top.

God does the same thing to us. He brings about circumstances in our lives that "heat us up," and guess what comes to the surface? Our impurities. If we fail to remember that God is bringing about our transformation and that He is using our children to reveal the selfish conditions in our hearts, then we will blame our children for our sinful actions. God wants us to understand and embrace this truth and deal with the dross properly.

"The heart is deceitful above all things, and desperately wicked; who can know it?" (Jer. 17:9).

God knew every mistake we would ever make when He picked us as parents. It's good to know He is not going to apologize to our children for picking us. It is imperative every time we do fail as parents, when we get angry and react in the flesh, that we take full responsibility. We need to go to the Lord and say, "God, I'm sorry. I blew it," and then to that son or daughter and say, "Honey, what you did was wrong, but the way Mommy or Daddy reacted was wrong too. Please forgive me." We must still discipline them, but we take responsibility for misrepresenting Jesus and ask for their forgiveness as well. That is how the dross is scraped off and we are transformed. If we do not do those two things, it is like taking a big spoon and stirring the dross back into us again, which is guaranteed to resurface again.

As I shared with you previously, my son Nicholas was one of God's greatest tools He used to reveal my evil, selfishness, and what an angry person I was. It was the greatest miracle to me when I was able to look at Nick when he made a mistake or challenged my authority and calmly say, "Poor choice!" without any emotion. I did not scream or yell or want to take his head off. It was great—praise God! God had proved Himself true. I had prayed for it, I had desired it; and once I began to take responsibility for my failures, I witnessed God's transformation in me.

Just as important as me seeing myself transformed, my son saw his daddy change right before his eyes. Yes—it took a season for this to take place. It did not happen over night. Today, Nicholas has strong faith and a healthy fear of God because he witnessed his father's transformation right before his eyes. This is one of the greatest testimonies in discipleship that you and I can give our kids.

"He will sit as a refiner and a purifier of silver; He will purify the sons of Levi, and purge them as gold and silver, that they may offer to the Lord an offering in righteousness" (Mal. 3:3).

God is purging us. He is heating us up and revealing our ugly, selfish conditions. We cannot run away from this process; we must embrace it and take responsibility in order for our transformation to occur.

If, after reading this material regarding loving your children, you have found that there is room for improvement, your first step must be admitting to the Lord, "I need help. I have failed. I need to change, God. I misrepresent You all the time. I'm sorry." Write out a commitment to bring change in the area of loving your children. In addition, I encourage you to pray about a time soon that you ask your children to forgive you. Loving our children is essential to successful parenting; we cannot allow anything else to take precedence.

CHAPTER EIGHT

God's Management Style

Thankfully, God has not given parents an impossible task because He has given us His Word and His Spirit. In His Word, He has given us specific instructions regarding raising our children and the Holy Spirit dwells inside us to empower us to do *all* things according to His will. He also revealed in His Word a management style, which we must follow if we desire His blessing on our endeavors. Our responsibility is simply to search His Word and obey what He tells us to do in His power and might.

What About a Single Parent

Again, I want to encourage any single parents at this point. Although these instructions may not apply specifically to your situation at this moment, it is highly likely that as a parent you will at some point give advice to other parents, and in order to be able to respond in a biblical fashion, you will need to know what God says about this subject. Additionally, you may end up married again some day. So please, as you read this chapter thoroughly, take it in as wisdom and understanding that God wants to teach you to help prepare you for what He may have planned in your life.

What About a Blended Family

If you are in a blended family marriage, please note that none of these instructions change; they apply to you as much as they do to the traditional family. Nowhere in His Word did God say if you are a blended family, you are excused from this management style.

As a Christian couple, you have agreed to embrace what God's Word says. If you adopt any other standard for family management, you are not under God's blessings. If we are disobedient to God's management style, there are consequences we bring upon ourselves about which He has pre-warned us for our protection. Of course, this is not a salvation issue, but a matter of having access to God's grace and power to intercede in and through our families.

The Institution of Family

As we discussed previously, the family is an institution, created by God, and, as such, in order for it to operate correctly, there must be leadership and authority within it. Let us look now to the structure God established for the institute of family:

"And the LORD God said, 'It is not good that man should be alone; I will make him a helper comparable to him'" (Gen. 2:18). Notice the word He used here is *helper*, not *leader*.

146

Further, we read, *"Therefore a man shall leave his father and mother and be joined to his wife, and they shall become one flesh"* (Gen. 2:24). So even though God said the man is to lead, He instructs that we are to see the relationship between husband and wife as *one*, unified. Just like a corporation is governed by customs through an organized management style, so is a family.

Remember, it is God's will and purpose we must submit to and follow, not our own or the world's. We are to trust the Lord and seek Him first. As we covered previously, we are *ministers* over our children, and, as such, we must be willing to abandon any of the traditions, cultures, cultural norms, ethnic traits, or personal experiences with our own parents, accompanying the way we were raised, that are contrary to God's ways. As such, it is solely God's Word that must govern us.

Many people I have counseled have said, "Well, in my culture, this is the way we do it."

I respond with, "Well, are you a Christian?"

"Yes."

"Well, then this time you must reject your culture."

As Christians, we must become oddballs. We are strangers, aliens to the world, and God's Word now dictates and governs how we do all things.

"If anyone comes to Me and does not hate his father and mother, wife and children, brothers and sisters, yes, and his own life also, he cannot be My disciple" (Luke 14:26).

Now Jesus is not saying in order to love Him that we have to *hate* our spouse or our children. Rather, if it comes to a choice between doing something God's way and what our parents want, the world wants, or what we believe is true, we must choose God's way. Basically the word translated in this verse as "hate" would be better translated " love less"; meaning that we must esteem God's Word and desires over and above what others may think and desire of us. Parents give their children bad parenting advice all the time. "My mother told me I should do it this way, not that way."

My response is, "So what? What say does your mother have over you now? The Word of God is your standard."

God Established the Authority Structure

God established the authority of the family, explaining that husbands, or fathers, are to lead the home. Understanding this, our goal must be to fulfill God's will and purpose, and to glorify Him.

> *But I want you to know that the head of every man is Christ, the head of woman is man, and the head of Christ is God.*
> — 1 Corinthians 11:3

> *Wives, submit to your own husbands, as is fitting in the Lord. Husbands, love your wives and do not be bitter toward them. Children, obey your parents in all things, for this is well*

pleasing to the Lord. Fathers, do not provoke your children, lest they become discouraged.
—Colossians 3:18-21

When our house functions in any other way, we are in direct disobedience to God. More specifically, the husband, or father, is to lead as God instructs, not in his own way, as a dictator with a heavy hand. Leadership in God's Word is laid out this way:

And a servant of the Lord must not quarrel but be gentle to all, able to teach, patient, in humility correcting those who are in opposition, if God perhaps will grant them repentance, so that they may know the truth, and that they may come to their senses and escape the snare of the devil, having been taken captive by him to do his will.
—2 Timothy 2:24-26

Christ showed that He was a servant; as fathers and husbands, we must have that same understanding. It goes right back to our strong foundation. As we rely upon God's strength, He gives us the ability to serve as Christ did, gentle to all, patient and humble.

"In humility" means without pride or arrogance. I know many men have taken on a dictator's attitude saying, "I'm the **man**, do what **I** say. I'm supposed to lead." But that is not the way God wants us to lead; that is the way of the flesh. On the other hand, a husband or father leading as Christ did is not passive or uninvolved. He does not relinquish his responsibility or authority to his wife in the area of training, as many men today are doing, saying to their wives, "I work; you take care of the kids." Meanwhile, their wives are thinking, "I wish this guy would step up to the plate! I've been hoping and praying that would happen."

I have an old dictionary which I like to refer to periodically, a big leather-bound *Webster International Dictionary* published in 1944. The word *husband* in that dictionary is defined as follows: "one who manages or directs his household, a married man, leadership and/or authority within a house, to manage prudently[1]." A 1996 version of the same dictionary, however, says: "a male head of household[2]." Period, that is it.

The word *management* in the 1944 version is defined as: "to conduct or direct, to handle successfully or cope with, to conduct, guide, administer, to render and keep one submissive, to guide by careful and delicate treatment, to treat with care, to *husband*[3]." Isn't that amazing? You will not find that in today's dictionary.

The Power of a Father

Fathers, I want to say this to you before I move ahead. It is so important that you truly understand the power that God has given you. It is supernatural. God has given you, as a father, power over your children that is absolutely beyond anyone else's influence.

For years, studies have proven the power of a father in the life of his kids. Many of these studies looked closely at the family dynamics in the lives of men like Sigmund Freud, Karl Marx, Adolph Hitler and many other hardened criminals. The one thing they all had in common was either no father or a very bad relationship with their father. On the other hand, when we study some of the most powerful people in the world, who have blessed our society, we see that most of them had healthy relationships with their fathers.

God has put this in the hearts of children to look instinctively to their daddies for affirmation and encouragement and value. But for some reason as we grow up and raise our own kids, we forget how influential our dads were to us, and we say things that are so harsh.

I have a huge sword in my office, a King Solomon sword; it is beautiful. I use it as an illustration when I am counseling. I say, "Dad, every time you get angry or frustrated at your child, it's just like you are pulling that sword out and slicing up the heart of your child."

When you act harshly toward your child, you are abusing that influential power God has given you. Your children know you are supposed to lead; they want you to lead, in all areas in your home, especially in the area of training them. That is why it is so important that you lead as Christ did.

Remember, moms, this is not about who is better, more important, or smarter. Among other negative things that Women's Lib has brought in is this notion of absolute equality between men and women. But God says a man should lead in all areas in our families.

Working in Unison

God has given my wife to me to complete me, and I know that since God said she is the one who completes me, I must look to her for input, especially in the area of the emotional condition of the hearts of my kids, which many times I do not see. Truthfully, I do not even care half the time.

When I come home and the chores are not done, I am thinking one thing and one thing only, "Hey, man, do it *now*. I don't care if you were up until 2:00 in the morning doing homework." I am ready to call down the discipline. I see things in black and white.

But my wife clues me into a bunch of information I did not know. "Honey, he was up until 2:00 because he's got finals this week. I told him he could do his chores tomorrow."

While I am still thinking, "The grass isn't mowed, and it needs to be done," Justin will come into the room and I am still sorely tempted to call him on it. But I do not, because my wife has helped me to see something I had not seen before. Now this does not mean that every time the kids want out of doing a chore or want to change a rule that they can just go to their mother and she has the power to make changes on a whim. So I bite my tongue, and say, "Hey, Justin, how was your day?" Because of my wife's input, Justin thinks I care about the stress he is under.

As men, we need to embrace how God made our wives—they often see things that we do not see. We would be foolish to say, "I'm the man, and it's going to happen *this* way." However, some men do exactly that. But that is not embracing what God says. Your wife completes you. You must endeavor to work together in unison.

There are, of course, times when I call the shots, and my wife has to submit to my authority. By doing so, she trusts God. Even when I am wrong, God blesses us, not because of me, but because my wife submits to my authority. When this happens, does she do it happily? Well, not always, but does she pout and frown and do all the other things some women do? Praise God! No, she has learned to trust the Lord with my authority, and, by doing so, she is blessed. When I set a rule and the disciplines, if she wants to change it, she knows she needs to speak to me first.

Most women are often dictated by their emotions. If they allow their feelings to rule in the area of training, many will not follow through consistently with enforcing the rule or issuing the discipline that follows. This is where men come in and say, "Honey, I understand they had a hard day, but discipline is what needs to happen." Training is about working together.

Resistance Brings Consequences

Let every soul be subject to the governing authorities. For there is no authority except from God, and the authorities that exist are appointed by God. Therefore whoever resists the authority resists the ordinance of God, and those who resist will bring judgment on themselves.

—Romans 13:1-2

153

Those who resist authority resist the ordinance of God, and rebel directly against the Lord. And by resisting this order, you bring divine judgment. God spoke these spiritual laws into existence; they are very similar to physical laws.

Gravity, for example, is a physical law. Gravity is a good thing; without it we would all fly into space and die. It keeps us down here on the earth with our feet firmly on the ground.

But what if you said, "I can't see gravity, so I don't believe in it. I believe I can fly"? If you climbed up on the roof and jumped off, what would happen? *Ouch!*

The spiritual laws work in the same way. When you say, "Well, God says I need to submit to the authority of my husband, but I don't care about that; I'm not going to try to embrace that," you may not have physical pain immediately, but you will have spiritual pain. The consequences are just as painful. When we choose to walk in the light, we have peace, joy, and contentment. When we don't, these gifts from God will begin to fade. Depression, un-fulfillment, and unhappiness will soon follow, along with the many possible physical ailments.

One couple I counseled: the wife looked like she had five hundred pounds on her back, she was all hunched over and looked depressed. She sat down and poured her heart out, how her house was a mess; she and her eighteen-year-old daughter were not speaking to each other; she and her fifteen-year-old son argued all the time; she was depressed, on medication, seeing a psychiatrist. She went on and on.

I looked at her husband, and said, "So, where are you in all this?"

"She's right. Our kids argue with her all the time."

I said, "What do you do about that?"

"Well, when she wants me to help, I help her. When she comes and gets me, I go in there and yell and say, 'Alright, that's enough.'"

Then the mom told me she knows that's not the right thing to do and explained why she was leading in the area of discipline rather than her husband, "My background is in psychology. I've been trained in this area." She said, "I can better deal with the children than my husband. I can communicate with them and talk things out."

I said, "You're depressed. You told me you feel like giving up and you're tired of the way you feel. Do you know why you are in this physical state? Because your home is out of order. You feel that way because you are supposed to. It's a direct consequence of disobedience to God's way. You're leading in the area of discipline, and your husband is supporting you. That's backwards. That's not the way it's supposed to be done."

From creation forward, the authority structure God has ordained for man is: God, man, woman, children. It does not have anything to do with inferiority. It simply means that the husband, not the wife, is the head of the home, especially involving the training. Think of it this way: dad—president, mom—vice-president. Does it hurt to think that way? If it hurts, you need to take it up with the Lord. You need to ask God to help you trust Him in this area. Husbands need to protect their wives here and lead.

What If Parents Disagree?

"Wives, submit to your own husbands, as is fitting in the Lord" (Col. 3:18). In other words, a wife is to submit to her husband's leadership, unless his leadership is in direct conflict with scriptural commands. For example, if your husband, who is not saved, tells you, "Don't talk to our children about the Lord," that is directly against scriptural requirements.

But let's say you have an unsaved husband who does not go to church, and you have a fifteen-year-old son who says, "Dad, I don't want to go to church anymore."

So Dad says, "Well, don't."

Should you discipline your son, become angry at him because he is choosing Dad's side instead of yours? Do you hold back affection? No. Just trust in the Lord and yield to the authority of your husband. I know it is hard to do but God's Word is clear. There is no exception. There are consequences when you try to undermine that authority.

What if you are the step-dad of a blended family, and there are rules being set in the home that your wife does not agree with for her biological children? The moment the wife says, "I don't like that rule; I don't think my son should have to do that," she's taken things out of God's hands and put them back in her own.

One of the main reasons so many blended families end in divorce is over disagreements regarding the training of the children. When they get married, they say, "This is my kid, those are your kids." However, there are no biblical grounds to that whatsoever. When you set your training, it is for *all* the kids living in your home.

The way the Lord tells us it should be done is: moms, when your kids challenge your authority as a mother, tell them, "This is what Dad wants."

When they respond with, "He's not my dad," you reply:

"That's right, he's not your father; you already have a daddy. I'm not trying to tell you he's your daddy, but when I married him, I embraced the authority structure in God's Word. And God's Word says that he must lead. I'm supporting him. If you don't like the rules and discipline, when he gets home, you can take it up with him. But in the meantime you need to accept this rule or discipline."

Win Your Husband

"Wives, likewise, be submissive to your own husbands, that even if some do not obey the Word [even those who do not proclaim to be Christians, or say they are Christians but do not act as such], *they, without a word, may be won by the conduct of their wives, when they observe your chaste conduct accompanied by fear"* (1 Pet. 3:1-2) emphasis added.

The most powerful thing that a wife can do according to God's Word is let your conduct (not your mouth) do the winning over of your husband. God tells a wife to put her trust in Him (God) and surrender to God's will, as a wife and He will do the work. The word *submissive* means a voluntary attitude of giving in, cooperating, assuming responsibility, and carrying a burden[4]. He is won by your chaste conduct, not your words or your rebellion. Chaste conduct means abstaining from all behaviors that are contrary to God's will as a wife toward your husband.

God wants you to work through this management system He has designed. To do so, you must be willing to yield to His authority.

Who Is Supposed to Lead?

The man is called to step up and lead, to be involved, to set the rules. He and his wife are to work together as a team, but he is the one ultimately responsible. It may be hard in the beginning if this has been out of order, but when you both understand this and you work toward it, you will be blessed. You will see God's intercession immediately, because God says He blesses obedience. Yes, it can be difficult, but it is ten times more difficult to do it wrong, because you are operating without the power of the Holy Spirit. God will not bless disobedience.

How do leadership roles get reversed? Let me give you a typical scenario. From the moment we brought little Nick home from the hospital, it was apparent that he was strong-willed and would be constantly fighting for control, and I took it personally, so I got angry.

My wife, on the other hand, saw this precious little boy looking up at me, while I was screaming like a maniac, and, as a typical nurturing mother, she instinctively wanted to protect her little baby from this big ogre. So she would step in, and then I would feel threatened and undermined. So we began arguing and undermining one another's parenting efforts until, finally, I gave up.

And that is typically the way it happens—it is usually the man who pulls away and lets his wife step up to the plate and have her way. This works for a little while, until one of two things happens. That strong-willed child becomes too much for her to handle, or adolescence, whichever comes first. Then the whole system starts unraveling, because that is not the way God intended it to work.

Some husbands have the attitude, "I'm the man, I make the money, and you take care of the kids. If you need my help, you let me know, and I'll just walk in there and roar." Others say, "Honey, my mom was in charge of discipline, so you should be the one who disciplines our kids." Dad only stepped in when the belt was needed. Men, we cannot relinquish the responsibility that God has given us. Both parents need to be willing to submit to God's plan, working together and using His management style.

How do you know if you have a problem in the area of management style? Take this short survey to find out:

1. Dads—when your children are in your presence, do you discipline them? Yes, no, sometimes?

2. Moms—do you consult your husband for input on all aspects of discipline? Yes, no, sometimes?

3. Dads—do you listen to your wife's input regarding the emotional state of your children? Yes, no, sometimes?

4. Moms—do you keep information from your husband regarding your children? ("We can't tell Daddy this because he'll get upset.") Yes, no, sometimes?

5. Dads—when Mom says, "No," and the kids come to you, do you always consult with your wife before responding? Yes, no, sometimes?

6. Moms—do you find yourself arguing with your teen, defending your reasoning behind a particular rule or disciplinary decision? Yes, no, sometimes?

7. Parents—have you sat down together and agreed on the rules and discipline you will use with your children? Yes or no?

8. Parents—do you disagree in front of your children over rules or discipline issues? Yes, no, sometimes?

Answers: 1-Yes, 2-Yes, 3-Yes, 4-No, 5-Yes, 6-No, 7-Yes, 8-No.

If your answers did not match these, there's a good chance your management style is out of order. How did you do? Most couples agree there is room for improvement in their management style. But what are the components of godly management in our homes?

Godly Leadership

First, a father is a servant-priest.

"Husbands, love your wives, just as Christ also loved the church and gave Himself for her, that He might sanctify and cleanse her with the washing of water by the Word" (Eph. 5:25-26).

". . . Called by God as High Priest 'according to the order of Melchizedek'" (Heb. 5:10).

Jesus is the high priest over the church; likewise, we are the priests over our homes. A priest has the authority and responsibility to perform the sacred rites or duties of a God ordained institution.

Men, when you are leading your family according to God's Word, you are not only serving God, but your wife and children as well. You do not have to attend seminary; the moment that you became a father, you were ordained by Christ to be a priest. He chose you, and He will empower you to accomplish this task.

> *So it was, when the days of feasting had run their course, that Job would send and sanctify them, and he would rise early in the morning and offer burnt offerings according to the number of them all. For Job said, "It may be that my sons have sinned and cursed God in their hearts." Thus Job did regularly.*
>
> —Job 1:5

This is one of the many scriptures that reveal the priesthood responsibility that God has given to us as fathers. Job took this responsibility to heart.

He continuously made sacrifices for his children. Likewise, we need to quit looking at our inabilities and our weaknesses, and start looking to God's promises and to the power that He has given to us that will enable us to accomplish this task.

A father is also a teacher and a manager. *"And you, fathers, do not provoke your children to wrath, but bring them up in the training and admonition of the Lord"* (Eph. 6:4).

A father is to be the leader in the training up of his children. Of course, moms are also a part of this process of training; when Dad is not there, she is in charge. But when Mom is bringing forth discipline, she is not doing it of her own accord, or because of what she thinks is right. She is following through with what she and her husband have worked out together.

". . . One who rules his own house well, having his children in submission with all reverence" (1 Tim. 3:4).

The word *rule* means "to manage[5]." A father sees that his children obey, including the authority he has left with his wife. When kids want to challenge the authority of your wife, you need to step in and say, "Poor choice. She is my helpmate and she has the authority to give you discipline for that action." The father is the main disciplinarian, the authority that ensures follow-through. If a child challenges a mother's authority, the father must make sure there is a discipline for that action.

Today, in most homes, the mothers are setting the rules and issuing the discipline, vindicating themselves in the process, rather than pointing to the father and supporting him in the training that he has set forth. Sadly, many mothers are missing the opportunities to comfort and nurture their children, especially after discipline, because they have taken on the lead role of the disciplinarian, contrary to God's plan.

So when the kids need to be nurtured after discipline, which is natural, Mom is not willing and open to do so, because she has the disciplinarian's mindset. She does not want to hug them, to sit down next to them and say, "I know this is hard, Honey." These moms miss thousands of opportunities that are so desperately needed along this whole journey of training up the children.

It is important to be open and available to comfort a child after discipline, as long as it is without compromise: you must still follow through with the consequence. You need to be available; you need to be ready to use those God-given gifts of nurturing and cherishing. If you have a disciplinary mindset, you may not. I am not saying fathers are not to be ready and willing to do the same comforting or nurturing if a child is looking for it. We fathers can and should be open and willing to do the same.

Single parents, you need to pray specifically, "Lord, I need to be able to switch hats. When I bring forth the discipline, I need to make sure that I'm ready to nurture and cherish my son or my daughter afterwards, without compromise. God, I know You will help me and give me wisdom here." And He will, because He loves you and your children. He will come alongside and empower you, because He loves your kids more than you ever could.

Many women, whose husbands do not care to be involved in training up their children, wonder, "Can I lead in this area?" Absolutely. But I say this to you: pray very specifically, "God, how can I help my husband believe he can do this?" Wives, you can be very persuasive. You know how to bless him and encourage him. Ask God to help you to approach your husband in a humble way to encourage him to take part in this area and to work together. Start off small. Most men really appreciate structure, especially when they can take part in designing it and overseeing it.

Dad, lead as God's Word says, as priests, using the management style that He has given you. Work together as a team and God will bless this process.

In following chapters, we will discuss specific aspects and tools in the training up of our children.

[1] *Webster's New International Dictionary of the English Language; Second Edition Unabridged*; G & C Merriam Company, Publishers, Springfield, MA 1944

[2] *Webster's II New Riverside Dictionary Revised Edition, Office Edition*; Houghton Mifflin Company, 1996

[3] *Webster's New International Dictionary of the English Language; Second Edition Unabridged*; G & C Merriam Company, Publishers, Springfield, MA 1944

[4] http://www.blueletterbible.org/cgi-bin/words.pl?book=1Pe&chapter=3&verse=1& strongs=5293&page=

[5] *Webster's New International Dictionary of the English Language; Second Edition Unabridg*ed; G & C Merriam Company, Publishers, Springfield, MA 1944

CHAPTER NINE

Teaching Them Biblical Truth

N ow that we understand the importance of a strong foundation in Christ, we have committed to loving our children, and are working within God's management style, we can properly engage in the training up of our children. Although many people believe that raising children is primarily about discipline, in truth there are two essential components of training up children. The first component of training is ***discipling*** your children (spiritual instruction) and the second component is ***disciplining*** your children (instilling character). As we review these two components of training, keep in mind the Lord wants you to implement them within the management style covered in the previous chapter.

Disciple Them

In an earlier chapter, we looked at how Moses instructed the Israelites in Deuteronomy 6:1-6, regarding the importance of their abiding relationship in God. After those directives, Moses continued instructing the Israelites, with respect to the raising of their children:

> *You shall teach them* [God's Words] *diligently to your children, and talk of them when you sit in your house, and when you walk by the way, when you lie down and when you rise up. You shall bind them as a sign on your hand, and they shall be as a frontal between your eyes. You shall write them on the doorposts of your house and on your gates.*
> —Deuteronomy 6:7-9 emphasis added

This passage declares that we are to teach God's precepts and commandments, His law, diligently to our children. That means not only must we be teaching through instruction, but also consistently living out the gospel. Sadly, less than 10 percent of parents in the body of Christ today are discipling their children. Instead, most Christians have left this up to the church or Christian schools. Did you know there is not one single youth group mentioned in the Bible? They did not exist. Do not get me wrong, I was a youth pastor, and I praise the Lord for youth pastors and the work that they do for kids. But somewhere along the line, we have determined that it is someone else's responsibility to instruct our children in spiritual things. But God said to you and me, as parents, that it is *our* responsibility to disciple our children, not the youth pastor's or anyone else's. They are here to assist us—not take our place.

"Teaching them diligently" also means we must be an example. In all our actions and deeds, we are to reflect the will of God, glorifying Him. Remember, hypocrisy breeds rebellion.

The truth is the most powerful way we can influence our children to put their trust and their life in the hands of Jesus Christ is by them witnessing the fruit of the Spirit in the lives of their parents.

I know one of the most powerful tools I have to exhort my children and teach them about Christ is the life my wife and I lead, how we exemplify Christ, how we act the way God wants us to act. And just as important as our actions is our transformation. When they witness us change or be transformed into the image of our Lord, this is one of the greatest tools of discipleship.

"Behold, children are a heritage from the Lord, the fruit of the womb is a reward. Like arrows in the hand of a warrior, so are the children of one's youth. Happy is the man who has his quiver full of them" (Ps. 127:3-5).

Our children are to be perceived as offensive weapons, like arrows. How many times have you watched an Indian in an old cowboy movie pull out an arrow and start defending himself? Never, because an arrow is not a defensive tool. An arrow is something you shoot *out*, away from you. It is an offensive weapon, to get your enemy before he gets you.

Most parents think, "If I can just get my kids through high school free from drugs and sex, I've won." But that is a defensive posture. God wants you to perceive your children as offensive weapons, not just defensive. You can never win a war if you only think defensively.

Think of it this way: imagine someone gave you a beautiful piece of land, completely clean, with the richest soil ever found, and said, "Here, this is yours, do whatever you want with it." But since you were not sure what you wanted to plant, you decided to wait a year or so and then decide what to do with it. How foolish would it be to believe that after a year went by, that piece of land would be in exactly the same condition as when you got it? What would be on that land? Weeds, growing and reproducing over and over again.

That is what the world is doing, constantly putting seeds of deception, lies, and bitterness into the soil of the hearts of our children. If you and I are not there tilling that soil and instilling God's Word into their hearts, then who is? Remember, no one has the power and influence that you and I have over our own children. God wants us to use that influence to instill His truth into the hearts of our children. It is our responsibility.

John 6:44 declares, *"No one can come to Me unless the Father who sent Me draws him."* Our children will not seek God or pursue spiritual things unless the Spirit of God is at work drawing them. Thankfully, it is not our responsibility to make our kids accept Christ. But it *is* our responsibility to be instilling God's truth into their hearts—what is right and wrong, what the Bible has to say about all things, who Jesus is, how one has a relationship with Him, and how to abide in Him each day.

When I was a youth pastor, parents would often call me, saying, "Hey, I don't know what you've been teaching my kid on Sunday nights, but he's been talking about God. I think you'd better sit down with him; I think he's ready to accept Jesus Christ."

My response was always, "Why are you calling me, telling me to do this? Why aren't you sitting down with him? Have you ever thought about leading your own kid to Christ?"

We need to seize those opportunities. As parents, we cannot make them Christians, but we must lead them to Christ to show them the opportunity He gives them to abide in Him.

The Opportunities for Discipling

Let's go back to Deuteronomy 6:7-9. The first instruction is *". . . talk of them when you sit in your house."* In order to talk to someone, what must we do? We must make time to communicate.

I was not always available to communicate with my children when they were young. You see, I used to race motorcycles; I still ride them, and I loved working on them when I was home. I'm a fix-it kind of guy. In other words, I always have some kind of tinkering to do around the house. So for years, on my way home I would think, "Which project am I going to work on tonight?" I would get home and immediately start on that project; meanwhile my little boys would follow me around, crying, "Daddy, Daddy." Within about twenty to thirty minutes, they would realize that I did not really want to have anything to do with them, so they would start playing by themselves or bugging my wife, because I was wrapped up in my projects.

We all get into ruts like this, and soon days turn into weeks, and weeks turn into months, and so on and so forth. Then one day they don't want to talk to us; instead many are turning to drugs, alcohol, or unhealthy relationships for comfort. Our children become teenagers, and now we are ready to talk to them, now we want all their attention. Thankfully, I did not let it get that far. I learned that when I get home, my real job begins.

Now, when I come home from work, I have no agenda other than being a servant to my family. My first priority is my home, not my work or my hobbies. At home, my ministry starts; so every day on the way home I pray, "OK, God, I'm coming home, help me to be a servant, help me to be available for my wife and kids."

So instead of jumping into a project right away, I go into the kitchen, and I would start making something to eat. Both my boys would run in and jockey for my attention. They would sit there for thirty minutes to an hour, telling me about their day. They knew that Dad was available to listen.

I also learned not to lecture at that time. At first, when Nick would launch into a story, I was quick to respond by lecturing him about what he should have done. But my wife helped me to see that they just wanted to talk while I listened.

On one occasion, Nick was telling me about a situation at school, something that was going wrong with a student he was having a problem with. When he was finished, I merely said, "Nicholas, what would be the right thing to do here? Maybe we should talk to this kid's dad."

"Dad, I can work this out on my own." He was not open for any input at that moment. Three days later Nick and that student ended up fighting, and both of them were suspended from school for two days. Instead of saying, "See, I told you so," I sat down calmly and said "Now Nick, if we would have done what we talked about the other night, the biblical way of handling this, sitting down with this boy's dad, his authority, and talking it out, do you think you would have gotten in a fight?"

"No."

"OK, you've got two days detention from school. During those two days, I have some projects for you to complete for your discipline."

So they do not always listen to our instructions. But those times are wonderful opportunities to train them and/or use as a life training exercise. However, you must be available, you must be approachable.

When your children become teenagers, you realize they are not pursuing you as often to discuss things with you. They do not want to talk when you want to talk. They start pulling away, and you have to learn to adjust. When my boys were older, I counseled two nights a week and I would get home late. But I learned that although I was tired, I still needed to be available for my kids. My first ministry is not the people that come in to see me, or the people that I go speak to, it is my family. Teaching them takes sacrifice; it takes a commitment, and for many teens, their time for talking is close to our bedtime.

"... *When you walk by the way* ..." (Deut. 6:7). God gives us plenty of opportunities to instruct our kids: driving in the car, working outside in the yard, camping, surfing, wherever you are. I remember plenty of times, surfing with Nick, sharing with him for forty-five minutes. It was like we forgot we were even on surfboards as we talked about God's creation and how wonderful He is.

I also remember the time I went camping with Justin and we talked about the whole concept of dating for hours and hours, or lying on the trampoline next to my daughter Katie, after jumping so long that my knees were killing me. There are so many great opportunities the Lord gives us to share His wonderful truths and promises with our children. I think some of the greatest Bible studies I had with my kids were not planned; they were just in the midst of life. We have to be mindful of every opportunity.

"... *When you lie down, and when you rise up*" (Deut. 6:7). Do you have a prayer time with your kids in the morning? If you feel you just do not have time, have you considered praying on the way to school?

When my kids became teenagers, we would pray at night as a family. They would come in our room, around our bed, and would pray together. And probably three nights a week, they were still there at 10:30

or 11:00 pm, talking our ears off. Let me tell you, it is a wonderful thing to have your teenagers wanting to share and talk to you. By trusting the Lord and applying these principles, I have watched God do something within my kids that is absolutely glorious. Today I am reaping the benefits of these things, and that is God's desire for you and your family also.

Scripture instructs us to: *"Be ready in season and out of season"* (2 Tim. 4:2). In other words, we need to look for opportunities at all times, being mindful of our responsibility to teach..

". . . That you may walk worthy of the Lord, fully pleasing Him, being fruitful in every good work and increasing in the knowledge of God" (Col. 1:10). This goes back to our foundation. Personally, I am terrible at remembering Scripture. I remember principles very well, but please do not ask me to quote a scripture; in many cases I will not be able to.

However, I can easily remember what I read in the morning throughout that day. And so many times issues would come up during the day with my children that were related directly to what I learned during my personal devotional time that morning! When the opportunities presented themselves I would remember what I had read and shared it with my kids. Consequently, my kids are convinced I am an amazing theologian. They think that I am smart. The truth is I am not! I merely have the right foundation.

"You shall bind them as a sign on your hand, and they shall be as a frontlet between your eyes"

(Deut. 6:8). A "frontlet" is a little leather pouch worn on the forehead. If you travel to Israel, you will see that many Jews still use frontlets today.

The frontlet served two purposes. It showed the people around you that you were a believing Jew and that you were meditating upon Scripture, because if you had something dangling in front of your face all day long, how could you forget? We too must be mindful at all times of our responsibility to disciple our kids, seizing the many opportunities that God places in front of us.

> *Blessed is the man who walks not in the counsel of the ungodly, nor stands in the path of sinners, nor sits in the seat of the scornful; but his delight is in the law of the LORD, and in His law he meditates day and night. He shall be like a tree planted by the rivers of water, that brings forth its fruit in its season, whose leaf also shall not wither; and whatever he does shall prosper.*
>
> —Psalm 1:1-3

Does that passage describe you? If you are putting God first, He will bless you, even in the times of difficulties and trials, so that your leaves will be green and you will be producing fruit—even in seasons of drought.

Monitoring Your Child's Interests

"Write them on the doorposts of the gates" (Deut. 6:9). That means all who enter your home, your friends

174

and your children's friends, your stuff and your children's stuff must glorify the Lord. Part of discipling our kids is monitoring the things that we allow in our home. God wants us to have a godly home.

> *And if it seems evil to you to serve the LORD,*
> *choose for yourselves this day whom you will*
> *serve, whether the gods which your fathers*
> *served that were on the other side of the*
> *River, or the gods of the Amorites, in whose*
> *land you dwell. But as for me and my house,*
> *we will serve the LORD.*
>
> —Joshua 24:15

Romans chapter 1 relates a long list of sinful behaviors that were going on at that time, and that are still going on today. Then Paul closes the chapter with: *"who, knowing the righteous judgment of God, that those who practice such things are deserving of death, not only do the same but also approve of those who practice them"* (Rom. 1:32). Now what this means, parents, is that you are guilty not only if you *do* these sins, but also if you find pleasure in *watching them.*

Parents often say, "When you're eighteen, you can watch this type of movie." But what is true for our children must be true for us as well.

One time a father came up to me after a parenting class and told me that he and his teenage son had gotten into a big argument over the music his son was listening to. His son said to him, "Well, Dad, what about your Pink Floyd albums? You listen to those once in a while. I've read the lyrics of some of those songs, Dad, and they are bad. They're no better than what I'm listening to." That father told me those Pink Floyd albums ended up in the trash, because he had learned that hypocrisy breeds rebellion.

Sadly, many Christians today pay more for their cable TV, which is 98 percent garbage, than they give in tithes. Just imagine what God will say to us when we stand before Him: "You paid $47.50 every month for cable that poisoned your kids' minds, and you gave how much to My church?"

Amazingly, many Christian parents sit right next to their children, laughing at shows full of sexual innuendos and destructive worldly philosophies. It is no wonder we have an epidemic today of young women "rooming" with guys—a disaster waiting to happen. Meanwhile, our media keeps pumping this type of philosophy into our kids' minds, and we open the door and let it in. We have to take a stand!

My wife received a copy of a women's magazine one time, and as I casually glanced through it, I happened upon an article about how to please your "man"; not your *husband*, but your *man*. That article was written pornography! Flat out pornography, in a women's magazine!

Ladies, you can read those types of articles and look at Victoria's Secret catalogs, and think they do not affect you, but they do. In truth, women check out women more than men do. But when you look at a beautiful woman's body, you are not thinking the way men do, you are not lusting. You are thinking, "I hate her, just wait until she has three kids."

But young men, or even boys, see something very different when they look at a woman dressed provocatively on TV. When I was young, the only thing we watched was Disney on Sunday nights. Can you imagine, back in 1966, sitting there watching Disney with your mom and dad, and a Victoria's Secret commercial comes on? My dad would have shot a hole through the TV, and someone at ABC would have heard from him for sure. That would have ended our Disney watching night.

Things have certainly changed. You pick up a newspaper today, and there are women in their underwear all throughout it; you do not have to be a peeping tom anymore, you just have to buy a newspaper.

If you look closely at the content of movies, you will find that PG13 movies often have ten times the amount of sex, sexual innuendo, and cussing as an R-rated movie. Satan knows exactly what he is doing to our kids. You must be aware of these things, and you have to know who you can trust.

My wife and I have certain Christian friends that we know we can trust with movie selection. Have I seen an R-rated movie? Absolutely. But I choose them carefully, based upon the content. Likewise, you need to decide, between you and your spouse and the Lord, what you will allow. Remember, hypocrisy breeds rebellion.

I walked into my son Justin's room when he was twelve, and he was playing a video game. Periodically, little captions would pop up when the characters walked up to each other. While I was watching over Justin's shoulder, all of a sudden a couple of cuss words popped up. I said, "Justin, what's that?"

177

"Oh, Dad, I don't read those."

"But wait a minute, how much of that kind of language comes up?"

"Well, they use it throughout the whole game."

I said, "Turn it off. Whose game is this?"

"My friend at school loaned it to me."

"I don't want to see it in this house again."

One time when Nick was a teenager, I came home and there were five kids in his room, laughing their heads off. They were playing his friend's video game. Nick called me into his room to see what they thought was so funny. The game featured a well-endowed woman in a hot-pants outfit kicking, shooting, and beating up all kinds of bad guys. The funny part was that while she was doing this, her breasts were bouncing all over the place. The boys were dying laughing. Although it did look funny, I told him it was not appropriate.

He said, "Wait, Dad, wait." He immediately went into the programming mode and changed the woman's breasts so that they were no longer bouncy. Then he did the same kick, showing me that her breasts did not move.

I said, "But Nick, why do you think they have that program? Because of the emphasis they're putting on it. Turn it off. Let's not have it in the house again."

The Internet is just as dangerous, if not more so, than video games. Make sure you have software to protect your kids (and dads) from pornography. From 1998 to 2003 more than 240 million pornographic web pages were added to the Internet, that's over 100,000 per day[1]. And every day the pornography industry is using the smartest people in the world to try to find ways around your protection.

Pornography is an epidemic amongst our teenage boys today, and it is just as addictive as heroin. We need to be in tune and involved. We need to watch the chat rooms they visit and monitor who they are communicating with. We need to get involved. I suggest you go into our website at www.parenting-ministry.org to learn about protective software to help you monitor this.

I Want My Privacy!

How many parents have heard, "Get out of my room"?

Back when Nick was thirteen years old, I was in his room one time, and we had a discussion going on about our rules on the type of music we allowed in our home. Finally he said, "OK, get out of my room."

I sat down in the corner of his room, and said, "What? Who said this was *your* room?"

He did not answer me, so I continued, "Nick, let me tell you where that lie came from: the pit of hell. I don't have a lease with you; you're not paying me rent. Nicholas, I am responsible for everything in this house. When I stand before the Lord when I die, you're not going to be standing next to me, saying, 'God, those were *my* CDs and *my* tapes, don't hold my dad responsible.' God's going to hold me 100 percent responsible for *everything* in this house. Yes, you have different interests, but if they don't meet the standard that I have set as a priest in my household, those things will never be in my house. And this room will never be yours. This room is mine. Because I love you, and you're my child, I allow you to live here. It doesn't matter if you're thirteen, Nicholas, or thirty-five, if you come live in my house, my standard will remain. So please, Nicholas, don't listen to that lie again. To think this is your room to do what you think is best for you is a lie from the pit of hell."

Our Commission

In the year 2000, statistics showed that when a mother of an unsaved family is the first one to accept Jesus Christ, there is a 17 percent chance the rest of the family will come to know Christ as well. When a father is the first one to accept Jesus Christ as his Lord and Savior, however, there is a 93 percent chance that the rest of the family will come to know Christ[2].

Dads, you have supernatural, ordained power from God; use it! Do not be tempted to relinquish your responsibility. When we go through these next principles, do not think in the back of your mind, "I can't do that. My wife is the spiritual leader, she knows the Bible better than me, so I'll just let her do it." It is not about you! This is what God has commissioned and ordained you to do, and He will empower you to accomplish it.

As parents, we must constantly evaluate ourselves biblically and be faithful to be obedient to Scripture in order to avoid hypocrisy when correcting our children. Remember, however, God is not looking for perfection, He wants transformation. If you are screaming and yelling, misrepresenting Christ, and you are not being responsible to ask forgiveness on an ongoing basis, this will definitely affect your ability to get your children's attention. God knows our failures, but are we following these principles to bring about the transformation?

Both parents are to be one in mind and judgment, in unity.

Now I plead with you, brethren, by the name of our Lord Jesus Christ, that you all speak the same thing, and that there be no divisions among you, but that you be perfectly joined together in the same mind and in the same judgment.

—1 Corinthians 1:10

". . . Fulfill my joy by being like-minded, having the same love, being of one accord, of one mind" (Phil. 2:2).

This principle applies to all two-parent families, including blended families.

Mom, if you have an unsaved husband, can you disciple your kids? Absolutely.

If you are a single mom, can you disciple your kids? Absolutely.

The Powerful Tool of Prayer

God's Word tells us we must *"pray without ceasing"* (1 Thess. 5:17). Consequently, fathers should pray with their wives and children every single day. Prayer is a powerful tool that God has given us; therefore we should incorporate it into our daily lives. Single moms, obviously, you can pray with your children in lieu of their father.

In my family, I am the only one who gets to hear my shy little daughter pray. She will not pray in front of my wife or her brothers. But let me tell you, my teenage daughter prays with more intelligence and intent than most adults: for God's strength, for forgiveness of her sins, for her friends and family, for people's salvation. I often get tears in my eyes as I listen. I have had the privilege of watching her grow into this young lady of prayer because every night, we pray together. I have made myself available. Then my boys come into my room, and we pray together, and it is powerful.

Instill God's Word

"But also for this very reason, giving all diligence, add to your faith virtue, to virtue knowledge" (2 Pet. 1:5). The Bible plainly tells us that we must be diligent to learn God's Word. To that end, family Bible studies should be done regularly, not when you happen to have time. You must make a plan and stick to it.

You can split your duties up, if that works for you. I have discipled my sons as they were growing up. My wife home schools and disciples my daughter. But on our weekly Bible study nights, she is in attendance. When I pray with her in the evenings, I ask her, "So what did you learn today in your Bible study?" Then I have opportunity to expound on some of the topics she brings up.

Seven Simple Steps for a Weekly Bible Study

• Simplicity

First, keep it simple. Remember, the objective is instilling God's Word in your children's heart; you are not trying to produce a Bible scholar. There are plenty of age-appropriate materials available to help you have a great little Bible study.

• Brevity

Second, keep it short. Family members have different attention spans. Be sensitive to the fact that the Bible study should be a fun family time, rather than a lecture.

When I started doing Bible studies with my kids, I was a youth pastor and my kids were very young. The first few times I did it, Nick would come in and be upside down on the couch and twisting around and throwing the pillow up in the air. I would get angry and frustrated, "Nicholas, sit up! Stop it! We're doing a Bible study now!"

Then I remember my wife telling me when we went to bed, "Honey, when you teach the high school, you have fun with them, so why, with your own kids, do you get all uptight?" I did not have an answer. So I learned to make our time together fun, not a lecture. Yes, chocolate shakes and popcorn is OK.

• Excitement

Third, try to make it exciting. Your goal is that your love and excitement for your faith will be transferred to your children. Are you excited about being in the Word? Are you excited about what God told you today? Are you excited to see the work that God is doing in and around you? If you are not excited, it will be a lecture every time.

When our boys were young they watched hours of a Christian animated video series of people in the Bible. My son, Nicholas, at the age of twenty-five, can still remember things he saw on those videos when he was a kid.

My daughter and I used to play Bible board games when she was young. Often we would play it three times in a row. We had some of our best hour and a half Bible studies that way. She'd pull a question and answer card, and then I was able to expound on the answers to the questions, and she just loved it.

- **Flexibility**

Fourth, be flexible. All families experience unexpected events. Your kids may start soccer or baseball, and you should not say, "No, you can't play baseball because Thursday night's our Bible study."

I think our family has had a Bible study on every night of the week at some point. Nick started a band; he had band practice, so we moved to Sunday nights. Then Justin got into volleyball, and he had practice; so we moved it to Tuesday nights.

You have to be flexible, but not so loose that any spontaneous event is a good excuse to postpone Bible study.

• Consistency

Fifth, be consistent. While flexibility is sometimes necessary, you must be consistent in your Bible study, thereby maintaining your commitment.

Oftentimes, parents go four or five months consistently, then summer comes and they go on a two-week vacation. When they get back, they think, "Oh, I'll start next week. Or the week after. Or maybe the one after that." Then suddenly there is a crisis going on in their house, and they realize it has been *months* since they had a study together.

God blesses obedience. Be consistent.

• Realism

Sixth, be realistic with your expectations. Teaching your children about God should occur over their lifetimes. Right now you are merely sowing seeds.

One father told me that he made his kids read a chapter every single day and write one full page on what it said to them. He was convinced that he was teaching his kids the Bible. But I could tell that his wife did not agree with his methodology. So I asked him what happened if they did not fill up the whole page, or if what they wrote was not acceptable. He told me that in those cases, he made them do it over. I said, "Do you think they enjoy that?"

We need to be realistic; adjusting our teaching style to the abilities and capabilities of our children.

• Get Started

Finally, and most importantly, do not put off starting. Change is always a bit uncomfortable; you may be nervous and afraid it will not go the way that you planned. In that case, go ahead and review the points above, but the main thing is to get started. Do not let your fears, your pride, your job, or your inabilities get in your way.

One summer, we simply used the *Daily Bread,* because things were so hectic. I had Justin read the Scripture verse, Nick read the story, we each gave our input, and we prayed. It was simple but effective.

To this day, I exhort my children to be in the Word on a continuous basis. I have taught them how to have a personal daily devotional life, but we all need to be encouraged once in a while. I still ask my grown sons, "Are you guys in the Word? How's your prayer life?"

When they were teens were they faithful every day? I do not really know. But when I saw them with their Bibles open, it just blessed me, because when I was a teenager, the last thing I ever picked up was a Bible. It never crossed my mind. I would have never made the time to do something like that.

Parents do not allow the world to dictate what your children believe. Make time to disciple your kids!

---

[1] http://www.family.org/socialissues/A000001155.cfm

[2] http://www.navpress.com/EPubs/DisplayArticle/3/3.11.32.html

CHAPTER TEN

Disciplining Our Children

Permit me to offer an illustration to help you understand why discipline is so important. A little nine-year-old boy was walking home from school one day and found a cocoon hanging from a branch. He had seen a video on how a butterfly emerges from a cocoon, so he broke the cocoon off the branch, brought it home, and put it in a jar with holes in the lid. Every day he would come home from school and stare at the cocoon—hoping he would be able to see this miracle take place.

One day he came home, and there was a small tear in the cocoon, and the butterfly was trying to wiggle out. So he sat for several hours, watching; but obviously a nine-year-old boy has a limited attention span. Finally, he could not stand it any more. He opened the jar, pulled out the cocoon, and began to carefully cut along the tear with a small pair of scissors. Once the cocoon was open, he pulled out the butterfly, but it looked very funny. The body was all fat, and the wings were all shriveled up behind it. It was so heavy, it could not even hold up its own weight.

He continued to watch, believing that eventually he would see this strange-looking thing turn into a proper butterfly. He even picked it up and tried to help it, but it would do nothing. Eventually it died right before his eyes.

That butterfly died because by God's perfect design—the struggle, the strain, and the difficulty of emerging from the cocoon forces the fluid out of the body into the wings. Then when it gets out into the atmosphere, the air touches its wings and dries them out, and it can then fly. By removing the struggle that God had put in place, the boy killed the butterfly, because it could not fly as it was designed to.

Likewise, by failing to discipline their children as God designed and commanded, many parents are preventing their children from growing to maturity. When you do not follow through with appropriate discipline, you do not instill the character traits that God wants your kids to have. And unfortunately, society pays for their immaturity.

Contrary to what many think, prisons are not filled with "bad people"; they are filled with average people who have never gained true maturity. A small percentage would be considered truly "bad." The rest simply never attained mature character, because their parents did not discipline them in the way they should have.

Training up our children is something God has called us to do. It is not always fun; in fact, it is often quite difficult. Just as butterflies do not struggle out of their cocoons thinking, "Oh, this is fun," our kids do not enjoy discipline either. Still, we must follow through.

Who's Making the Decisions Around Here!

If we put the age of our children on one side of a graph and compared it to the number of decisions they made versus the number of decisions we, as their parents, made for them, we would see that in the beginning, all decisions are made by parents, which is logical. When our kids come home from the hospital, they are obviously not yet capable of choosing for themselves. But at some point on the graph, those lines would cross and continue until our children are making all of their own decisions.

In other words, as our children are getting older, our goal is for them to begin making healthy, wise decisions; and we want to get to the point where we are no longer making decisions for them. Now you can look at this graph and think, "Of course, that is just common sense." But if you do not have a plan in place, and a method of training your children to make the decisions, this will not happen. You must have a plan in place.

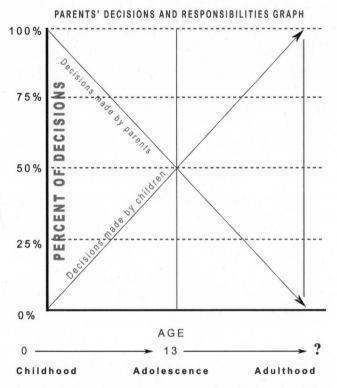

A-1

DISCIPLINE FOR RAISING ADULTS

PARENTS' DECISIONS AND RESPONSIBILITIES GRAPH

Decisions made by parents

Decisions made by children

PERCENT OF DECISIONS

100%

75%

50%

25%

0%

AGE

0 ⟶ 13 ⟶ ?

Childhood   Adolescence   Adulthood

If you don't know where you are going you will probably end up there!

Training Versus Controlling = Growth Versus No Growth

At this point, it is important to note that God has instructed us to *train up* our children, not *control* them. The difference between the two is mainly a mindset of how we perceive our job as parents. *Controlling* means to exercise power over, to dominate or rule, to restrain, a restraining force[1]. A controller is a dictator, not a trainer. He will not accept failure. A controller's perspective is that failure is wrong or bad and is a direct threat to his parental authority. A controller is motivated by self-fulfillment, not God's will. He takes his children's failures personally, as deliberate, as if they were purposely trying to hurt him. He is more concerned about what others think than about what is right. (Keep in mind that a woman is just as likely to be a controlling parent as is a man.)

Have you been told by your spouse that you are controlling? Have you been told that you are legalistic, that you have unrealistic expectations for your kids? Many times this behavior is a result of how you were raised, perhaps never feeling you lived up to your parents' expectations.

If you are harsh and controlling, you must ask God, "Why do I perceive my kids' failures this way? Why am I responding and reacting in this way? Is it because I have not forgiven my own parents?" It is essential that you deal with this issue.

Defiance Versus Foolishness

Failure, even willful disobedience, is *not* the same as defiant rebellion. If you believe it is, you will respond to your children in the wrong way, usually in the flesh. Defiant, rebellious behavior is when your children refuse to receive the discipline that follows their foolish acts of immaturity. If you do not understand this truth and know the difference between defiance and foolishness, you are likely to hurt your children by making them feel unloved through your negative communication attached to your discipline.

Mistakes are not defiance, even if your kids have been repeatedly told what not to do. Mistakes are simply immaturity, foolishness. God clearly explains that children are foolish, and that we are here, to train them.

> *The Lord's bond-servant* [that's us] *must not be quarrelsome, but be kind to all, able to teach, patient when wronged, with gentleness correcting those who are in opposition, if perhaps God may grant them repentance leading to the knowledge of the truth, and they may come to their senses and escape from the snare of the devil, having been held captive by him to do his will.*
> —2 Timothy 2:24-26, NASB

Training Means . . .

Training means to cause to grow as desired, to make or become prepared or skilled[2]. God's best is the trainer's motivation, not his own desires or expectations.

Let me give you an illustration. If you had a two-year-old tree in your backyard with a trunk about three inches in diameter that had a forty-five degree bend on it, wouldn't it be foolish for you to grab the tree and forcibly straighten it up? What would happen to that tree? It would snap right off at the base, and you would end up destroying it.

A trainer, like a farmer, which means husbandman[3], knows that when he finds a bent trunk, there is a proper way and an improper way to fix, which means train, the tree. The improper way would be to force the tree upright immediately thereby causing much damage, possibly destruction, of the base of the tree. This is an example of controlling. The proper way would be to train the tree by putting a light amount of pressure against the tree in a pre-determined direction to straighten the tree. As the tree conforms to the pressure, then gradually more pressure can be applied in the same direction until the tree will eventually be in the desired position and no longer "bent". This is an example of training.

That is the way we need to perceive our kids. They come to us bent. Have you not noticed? We do not like them bent; we want them straight right now! Because they are "bent" and they act their normal age, when we get angry we confuse them by saying, "Don't act that way!"

God wants us to understand how to perceive our job and what our mindset toward training should be. We must have an understanding that failure and foolishness are expected and normal, merely part of the whole journey.

"And you, fathers, do not provoke your children to wrath, but bring them up in the training and admonition of the Lord" (Eph. 6:4). The word translated *"bring them up"* is *ektrepho,* which means bring up to maturity, to train or educate. This must be our goal

193

for our kids in the area of discipline: to raise them to maturity.

The word "training" here means discipline, chastening, correction, educative discipline, i.e., discipline that regulates character." We are instilling character in our children's lives. This is the means by which we carry out the goal.

"To bring up" is the goal; "training" is the method by which we reach that goal.

The last part of this verse, "admonition of the Lord," means instructions, warning, exhortation, any words of encouragement or reproof that lead to correct behavior as unto the Lord, or as the Lord instructs us to, not in our own way.

Born Foolish

"Foolishness is bound up in the heart of a child" (Prov. 22:15). The word "foolishness" means this: "deficient in understanding, unwise, brainless, irrational, ludicrous, a lack of judgment[4]." Does that not perfectly describe our children? They are lacking character maturity. So why do we get so angry when they act foolish? God's Word declares they are born that way! Instilling character is like training your muscles.

Think of it this way: imagine you are a coach, your children are the members of your team, and the goal is to get them bench pressing two hundred pounds. So when your students show up every Monday, Wednesday, and Friday, your job is to train them to bench two hundred pounds. If the first day they arrived ten minutes late, and you spent the full forty-five minutes lecturing them, what did you do toward training their chest muscles? Nothing. What if you yelled and screamed and threatened to take away everything they had? Still nothing.

Until you lay them on the bench, doing bench presses with lighter weights, there will be no training taking place. Discipline means training them every time that they fail, every single time. How often do they give us opportunities to train them? We need to have a biblical perspective toward our children's foolish behaviors . . . to see them as an opportunity to discipline or train them to get closer to our goal of raising them towards maturity.

Let me give you another illustration. If you dropped two hundred pounds on your ten-year-old's chest, and he just lay there, immobile, would you yell, "Pick it up, what's wrong with you? Come on, you should be able to do this"? Of course not, because you know that a ten-year-old cannot bench press two hundred pounds. We need to view their failures or foolishness as a sign to us and them that their training is not yet complete. If we become angry or aggravated we are sending the message to them that we expect them to be mature now as in bench press two hundred pounds now. We are also revealing to them, if we react to these training opportunities in a negative way, that they are not valuable to us.

We know it is a process to develop muscles so we begin with lighter weights, gradually increasing the weight as your child demonstrates the capacity to lift more, until eventually he achieves the goal. In the same way in which a muscle grows or increases in strength ever so slightly every time he lifts the lighter weight off his chest. A child's character grows just slightly every time he is disciplined. So when your kids fail and act foolish, why do you scream and yell, act disappointed, and get upset? They have merely proven to you that they cannot bench press two hundred pounds at that moment. They do not have the character yet. Do you see the difference?

Mature Character Defined

Of course, in order to instill mature character in our children, we must first decide: what is our definition of maturity? What is our goal? What is the bull's-eye that we want to aim at? There are three components to the bull's-eye of maturity.

First, we must instill in our children morals and values, an understanding of right versus wrong. Previously we discussed the importance of discipling our children and instilling God's Word into their hearts. God even instructed our father of the faith, Abraham, to do this to his son:

> *For I have known him, in order that he may command his children and his household after him, that they keep the way of the LORD, to do righteousness and justice, that the LORD may bring to Abraham what He has spoken to him.*
>
> —Genesis 18:19

Second, we must teach our children personal responsibility—the ability to take care of themselves, to follow through on things they have committed to do, or the things required of them, without anyone else having to prompt them.

"And let our people also learn to maintain good works, to meet urgent needs, that they may not be unfruitful" (Titus 3:14).

"The sluggard craves and gets nothing, but the desires of the diligent are fully satisfied" (Prov. 13:4 NIV).

Third, our children must learn self-control—the ability to govern themselves emotionally, physically, and spiritually; the ability to not always yield to the path of least resistance.

Proverbs 29:11 illustrates the emotional side of self-control: *"A fool vents all his feelings, but a wise man holds them back."*

2 Peter 3:17 describes the physical side of self-control: *"You therefore, beloved, since you know this beforehand, beware lest you also fall from your own steadfastness, being led away with the error of the wicked."*

These three simple principles—morals and values, personal responsibility, and self-control—are our bull's-eye. This is what we are to be instilling in our children. Do you know that every foolish act your son or daughter has done to date and will do in the future falls under one or a combination of these three characteristics? Why? Because they were born without them. It's our job to train them.

It is so important that you see this, because if you do not know where you are going, you will most likely end up someplace you do not want to be.

This also brings unity between husbands and wives; working together for a clear, common goal. And if you do not have a clear goal, how are you going to measure your success?

If a corporation says, "We want to sell three million dollars worth of product," it would be wise to, once a quarter, take stock, asking, "Are we close to our mark?" It would be reckless and irresponsible to wait until the end of the year to measure their success. Likewise, if you have clear goals for training up your children, you will be able to measure your success. In a later chapter you will learn how to implement a procedure which will help you and your children see how close you have come to your goals.

That way, when your children ask for more freedom in a certain area, you can merely look at the amount of disciplines they have received recently, and it will be obvious whether or not they have earned the freedom they are seeking. You will not have to convince them; instead you can calmly say, "Let's have a few months of consistency in this area, and then we'll talk about it, OK?"

So your answer is not based upon how you feel at the moment, but upon practical, realistic criteria that everyone can see.

Our Kids Need to Know

Proverbs 23:7 says, *"For as he thinks in his heart, so is he."*

When I was fourteen years old, I had a distorted view of what a man was: being a tough guy, using drugs, and having many girlfriends, so that is what I went after. How foolish! But no one ever told

me the truth. No one ever gave me a bull's-eye to shoot for.

I interview hundreds of teenagers a year, and less than 5 percent even come close to giving a proper definition of what a mature adult is.

When I ask them, "When do you think you should know?"

Most respond with, "I don't know."

I then ask them, "Does something suddenly just happen, and you become an adult when you move out?"

The common answers are "I don't know. I guess when you get a job, or when you move out, or maybe when you get married and have kids. I don't know."

It is our responsibility to tell them! It is no wonder our generation of teenagers is so lost; the world is telling them what is important and where the bull's-eye is: public schools, media, music, television shows, Internet, books, and magazines. Satan is bombarding our children with lies, confusion, and misdirection. This is why it is so important for us parents to define clearly both our goal of maturity and the method we are going to use to get them there.

---

[1] *Webster's New International Dictionary of the English Language; Second Edition Unabridged*; G & C Merriam Company, Publishers, Springfield, MA 1944

[2] *Webster's II New Riverside Dictionary Revised Edition, Office Edition*, Houghton Mifflin Company, 1996

[3] *Webster's New International Dictionary of the English Language; Second Edition Unabridged*; G & C Merriam Company, Publishers, Springfield, MA 1944

[4] *Webster's New International Dictionary of the English Language; Second Edition Unabridged*; G & C Merriam Company, Publishers, Springfield, MA 1944

CHAPTER ELEVEN

The Four Tools of Training

Now we come to implementation. How do we train up our children to maturity? Before we continue into the practical aspects of discipline, it is important that you understand there is a proper sequence that must be followed in training up your children. Please note the order in which we discussed the issues of discipling and disciplining.

Discipling must be in place before disciplining begins. Remember, *"As he thinketh in his heart, so is he"* (Pro. 23:7). In other words, until the heart is transformed, the behavior will not change either. Unfortunately, parents spend most of their time trying to change the *"so is he,"* the behavior, rather than the heart. The heart is only changed by love and discipleship. You cannot emphasize the discipline component and minimize the love and the discipleship components.

"As in water face reflects face, so a man's heart reveals the man" (Prov. 27:19).

Morals and values are taught by example but also by instruction. The example of our life, how we treat our children (in a loving way and discipling them), is God's way to train and instill biblical morals and values in the hearts of our children. When this is not the main emphasis and we are not doing this according to God's Word, parents can be the greatest tool of the enemy to harden the hearts of their children, so that when the seeds of God's Word are given to them or the seeds of any correction, it will lay upon their hearts like hard ground and not penetrate and take root.

Why Discipline?

Parents must discipline their children for the following reasons:

> God commands it (Prov. 23:13-14; 22:6).
> It demonstrates love (Heb. 12:6).
> I used to work with teens in juvenile hall, and I was amazed at how many kids, although they had never set foot in a church or opened a Bible, said, "I know my parents didn't love me because they never disciplined me." Kids know instinctively that discipline is part of love. God puts that in our hearts.
> We are raising adults not children (Ps. 32:9). We must train them to become mature.
> It produces peace in the home (Heb. 12:11).

To teach them personal responsibility and self-control, there are four basic principles or tools we should use.

Tool Number One: Written Rules

First, we must establish boundaries, or rules, which must be clearly written out. Many parents tell me, "My kids know what the rules are," but I have proven so many of them wrong! I ask the parents to tell me the rules, then I bring the kids in, and most of the time they give me more rules than their parents did. The reason is, so often the parents shout out, "If you ever do that again, such and such will happen." After a while they forgot they even said it; but the kids do not. Rules need to be clearly written out. God gave us a great example to follow.

"So He declared to you His covenant which He commanded you to perform, the Ten Commandments; and He wrote them on two tablets of stone" (Deut. 4:13). God wrote His commandments on stone! He knew we needed something written down. He governs the whole world with just these ten rules; in most homes you can get away with less than ten rules.

Rules must be written out for the following reasons:

- Written rules reduce confusion for both parents and children alike. Clear policies are important, any good manager knows that. If you do not have clear policies, everyone underneath you will do whatever they want.

- They help build and maintain unity between parents, promoting a team spirit.
- They remove double-mindedness and unfairness. Parents frequently make the mistake of giving their five-year-olds ("the baby" of the family) unfair mercy compared to their eight-year-olds ("you're older, you should know better"). Also, many parents let their emotions at the moment dictate if they want to enforce a rule or not. This makes things both unclear and also unfair.
- They keep us from being inconsistent. We are more apt to follow through if the rule is written down.

Tool Number Two: A Predetermined Discipline

A Predetermined Discipline—The Training, the Consequences if a Rule Is Broken.

Discipline means to train: it is positive, it is good, it is an act of love. *Training* means to instruct, to correct, to mold and perfect (see section in chapter 10 titled: "Training Versus Controlling").

"Because the Lord disciplines those he loves, and he punishes everyone he accepts as a son" (Heb. 12:6 NIV).

This principle has been in the Bible from the beginning of time:

Behold, I set before you today a blessing and a curse: the blessing, if you obey the commandments of the LORD your God which I command you today; and the curse

[or a consequence] *if you do not obey the commandments of the LORD your God.*
—Deuteronomy 11:26-28 emphasis added

We must give our children clear boundaries and if they cross them we must discipline them. We must view their failure as an opportunity to train them.

In sports we use this principle all the time: in football if you step out of bounds, you cannot go up to the referee and say, "I didn't mean to, I'm sorry." and expect him to excuse you from your consequence. Rather, the referee is going to proceed with the discipline for that infraction by marking the ball down where you stepped out. It is not negotiable. Whether you were hoping to get away with the infraction or it was simply an accident does not matter or change the predetermined consequences.

The discipline should be predetermined and not thought up at the moment. Let me give you an analogy. Suppose one of your rules is "no jumping on the couch." One morning you walk past the living room and out of the corner of your eye you see your little seven-year-old, your compliant one, jumping on the couch. You think to yourself, "I don't want to deal with that right now, I haven't had my coffee yet," so you pass right by into the kitchen.

Once you have had your two or three cups of coffee, you are feeling much better. It is time to get ready for church and you are trying to rush everyone to get ready. You walk by the same doorway, and now there is your nine-year-old, the strong-willed one, doing the exact same thing—jumping on the couch. However, instead of ignoring the infraction this time, you say, "I've told you so many times not to jump on that couch!" and you spank him soundly.

That was not a predetermined discipline; that was spontaneous punishment (I'll explain the difference next) based on how you felt at the moment and the panic of the situation. This type of emotional parenting creates jealousy between siblings and often convinces many strong-willed children, who will naturally receive more discipline, that their parents love them less than their brother or sister.

Tool Number Three: Punishment—The Motivator

Thirdly, we must also be willing to bring forth punishment. *Punishment* simply means "a measured amount of pain to motivate[3]." Punishment is part of the overall discipline plan, but it is different from a discipline. Punishment is the motivator to encourage our children to yield to the parents' authority and accept the discipline.

Read that description of punishment again. Do you see anything regarding words of anger, yelling, cussing, disgust, judging, comparing, ignoring, or pouting in that description? No, you do not. So many of us believe that our discipline will not work unless we are angry and raising our voices. That, however, is a worldly philosophy that has no place in Christian homes.

"Do not withhold correction from a child, for if you beat him with a rod, he will not die. You shall beat him with a rod, and deliver his soul from hell"

(Prov. 23:13-14). This verse often generates confusion. He is not telling you to go out and beat them. Rather, it is an idiom in which the rod represents two things, a measuring tool and authority.

Yes, God is telling us, "Some kids need pain in order to grow," but He is not telling you to grab a stick and beat them. You must take the whole Word of God as His counsel. God's Word is not contrary to itself.

I must admit, there were times I enjoyed spanking Nicholas, but when it came to Justin (who I spanked less than five times in his entire life) and Katie, (who I spanked once) it broke my heart. It was one of the most difficult things I ever had to do as a daddy—to look down at my little brown-eyed girl as she looked up at me with that expression of, "Daddy, what are you doing?" But when she would not yield to my authority and accept the discipline, I had to follow through. It was hard for me to follow through, but I had to do it, because she was testing my authority and refusing the discipline.

"No chastening seems to be joyful for the present, but painful; nevertheless, afterward it yields the peaceable fruit of righteousness <u>to those who have been trained by it</u>" (Heb. 12:11 emphasis added). I am sure you have heard the saying, "This is going to hurt me more than it's going to hurt you." Perhaps your parents said it to you. This is where it came from. Punishment is given to a child only if they refuse the discipline that follows the breaking of a rule.

There is a great deal of confusion about the whole spanking issue. Spanking is the most common form of punishment for children under the age of eight years old. Some parents have told me, "I don't believe in spanking." But as Christians, God's Word tells us that if a child will not yield to the predetermined discipline, then we need to find a way to motivate them. You may have had parents who beat you within an inch of your life, or they never spanked you at all. What they did wrong should not dictate our obedience to God's Word. If you do not spank your child, if necessary, you will pay dearly later. That is not my opinion; that is what Scripture says.

I have been working with parents long enough to see the same strong-willed three-year old whose parents said, "We don't believe in spanking" turn into a fourteen-year old engaging his father in a fistfight, along with many other irresponsible and rebellious behaviors. I am telling you, if a child is unwilling to accept the discipline, then we must find a way to get them to yield and accept it. When you have been blessed with a strong-willed mule, they have to be motivated sometimes.

When I was about eleven years old, I was a daredevil. My friends and I used to jump flights of stairs down at the high school on our bikes. When we finally succeeded at one flight, of course I had to try two flights. So I did, and crashed, tearing up my knees and bending both my wheels. I was in serious pain! But I still rode my bike home. I fixed the tires and was back on my bike the next day. You bet I didn't go back and try to jump both sets of stairs again.

Today, when I drive down the road and I see someone on a bicycle, believe me, I do not have a flash back to when I hurt myself on my bike; I do not experience some kind of emotional trauma. This is what worldly psychology has led us to believe will happen if we spank our kids.

Certain strong-willed kids need to be motivated. They do not like the idea that you are the authority. Remember God made them strong-willed and they often want to rule and run the household. Sometimes they need those motivators to get them to yield to your authority and accept the predetermined discipline.

Pain is a good thing, it is part of life, and it teaches us. Just like me learning not ever to jump two flights of stairs on my bicycle again. Pain has taught me, in many areas, what I can and cannot do as a person.

This is how a predetermined discipline is used in the overall discipline process: let's say your rule is no jumping on the couch; the predetermined discipline for, let's say, a five-year old is a five-minute time-out in a chair. If he refuses to sit in the chair until the five-minute timer goes off, then your child is asking for the motivator. After a spanking (see: Principles in Spanking in Chapter 14), put them back in the chair and restart the timer at five minutes. No anger, no yelling, no threatening. It is a simple process.

Understand: punishment in itself does not train. Many parents do not know the difference between punishment and discipline, and their kids do not know either. Why is it that over 80 percent of the people who go to prison end up back in prison[1]? Because the whole system is designed on punishment, not training. The moment they are out and "Big Brother" is off their back, and the fear and the motivation are gone, they go right back to their former behavior. They have not learned anything. Punishment is just the motivator to receive training. You must not lose sight of this truth.

Tool Number Four: Consistency

We must be consistent. If I took a survey of how many people drive above the speed limit, if people were honest, the results would show that virtually everyone speeds at one time or another. If I asked each person why they speed, they would say, "Well, because everyone else does," or "I'm always late," and so on and so forth. But the real reason people speed is not merely a lack of self-control, but the inconsistency of the police department in enforcing the rule.

What if they put computer chips in our cars, and no matter where we were, if we went one mile an hour over the speed limit, it would send a signal to the police department, and three days later we got a ticket in the mail? What would happen to our bad habit? We would suddenly find that we have self-control, because we do not like those types of disciplines.

Kids are no different. Consistency is important. If there is no consistency, it is as if there are no rules and no training, and it equals no peace. Being consistent will not make our children stop being foolish overnight. Remember, we are instilling character into them every time we give them a discipline when they cross a boundary (break a rule). It is like a muscle that is exercised; every time you discipline (train) your muscle, it grows just a little each time.

Consistency can be learned for moms, who are inconsistent because they are emotional beings. Moms, do not apologize for your emotions, just do not compromise God's will because of them. God did not give you that gift for you to use it wrongly. He gave you a nurturing heart, that is good, but you cannot allow your emotions to dictate your obedience to Christ and your husband, in terms of following through with disciplining your children.

If you are not consistent, you are teaching your kids to become manipulators and that everything is negotiable. Worse than manipulative kids, however, is the fact that they are going to become adults and go into the work force believing and practicing the same concept, and society is going to suffer. Remember, God's view is: discipline is loving our children. Now, I know there are men who also struggle in this inconsistency too. Work together and pray for each other. Ask God to help you to be consistently obedient to Him in this area.

Don't Count

Many parents, especially moms, use counting as part of their discipline: "Stop doing that! I'm going to count to three, and you'd better stop!" But counting is a destructive component of disciplining. Have you noticed that strong-willed kids cannot stand the idea that you are the boss? When you tell a strong-willed child not to do something, the first thing in his mind is, "I've got to win here. I've got to prove to myself and my parents that I'm in control."

So he will go up to something that you have already told him not to touch, make sure you are watching, then reach out and come ever so close to touching it. Once you start with, "Don't you dare, don't you touch that," they have your full attention. Then you continue with, "I'm going to start counting. One . . . you'd better get . . . two . . . two and a half . . . I'm telling you!" By this time your veins are popping out and you are ready to explode. And your little mule merely says to himself, "See, I really am in control, I just consumed three minutes of her time, and look how angry I got her. I'm in control!" This destructive component of discipline provokes strong-willed children to continue to try and rule over you.

Instead, you merely say, "Get away from that now." If they do not immediately move away, give them a discipline. Follow through with whatever the discipline is. Do not let yourself be sucked into these emotional scrimmages that will get out of hand when they become teenagers if you don't stop it now.

Let's Make a Deal!

Remember the show *Let's Make a Deal?* I loved that show! When people picked a particular curtain and won motorcycles in the back of a truck or something, I thought, "How cool, I want to be on that show!"

Kids view our training them in the same way and believe everything is negotiable. Let me explain using the following table and explanation: door number one is "follow rules"; door number two, "break rules, accept the discipline"; door number three, "no rules, no discipline." If given the choice, which door would our children choose? Of course they would choose number three if it is available.

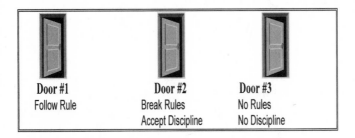

Strong-willed children will pick door number three. More compliant children, like my son Justin and my daughter Katie, will more often than not choose between doors one and two. Compliant kids have an inner desire that motivates them to operate within boundaries of doors one and two. You see, it is very important to them that they please you and you are pleased with them. Nick, on the other hand, often could not have cared less whether we were happy or not; he just wanted to be in control.

So do yourselves a favor, get a pen or pencil and put a big "X" over door number three. If your kids have been choosing door number three on a continuous basis and you have been flipping out, do not be surprised anymore, because you know that they are going to try it. Instead, explain to them and show them by day-to-day example that door number three is no longer an option.

As a matter of fact, you can use this illustration. Sit down and talk to them about their choices. Then when they start the behavior, you simply remind them, "I know you want door number 3, don't you? Remember our meeting? But it's not happening. Do your discipline or you are asking for a motivator."

Don't we approach life the same way? If we could get away with it, we would not behave all the rules either. I have been a "desert rat" for over thirty years. When I see those signs out in the middle of the sand dunes that say "closed area," I get so irritated. What are they trying to protect, a lizard? I have been camping out there for thirty years, and here I am paying taxes so they can put signs up that say I cannot go into areas that I have been riding through for years. There is a side of me that rebels against this even as an adult.

Adapting Our Training Without Compromise

"Train up a child in the way he should go, and when he is old he will not depart from it" (Prov. 22:6). "The way he should go" means every child is unique in their personality, meaning some may need more discipline, tighter boundaries, and tougher discipline than others. This verse also means that we parents must be willing to adapt to our children's personality or bent.

When Nick was in school, it was very typical for us to have two, maybe three teacher conferences a year. We were ready for it, most of the time, waiting for that call: "Mr. and Mrs. Caster, can you come down—we need to have a little meeting with you about your son, Nick." So we would go meet the teacher and hear about his behavior issues.

One time, when Nick was probably in the third grade, we sat down with his teacher—who was newly married with no children—and she began telling us about Nick's behavior in class. When she was finished, she asked us, "Do you guys discipline?"

"Well, sure we do."

But we could tell by her expression she thought we were lying, or that we did not know what we were doing. She ignored what we had said and continued, "It's really important for parents to set boundaries," then proceeded to give us advice.

I could tell my wife was getting upset, so I kind of jumped in, and said, "Look. I know Nick likes to run everything; it's his personality. Nick is strong-willed. Yes, we have rules at home. But you just told me this has been going on for several months, and we're just hearing about it now? Let's bring Nick in, let's go over what he's doing, let's agree on a discipline that you can give him here—like picking up trash during lunch or PE. Let's find some way that you can communicate to me when I pick him up, and then we will follow through with additional discipline at home."

That is my son. If he did not feel like doing math, he would simply interrupt the whole class, shouting out, "Who wants to go out and play?" That was just the way he was. Today, he has taken that strong will and directed it in the right way. But believe me, when we were raising him, it was not fun.

Two years after Nick, the same teachers would get my second son, Justin—my prince, the straight-A people-pleaser, writing little notes on the bottom of his papers, "I love you; you're the best teacher."

At Justin's sixth grade graduation, the teacher brought each child up, and said something nice about them. When she got to my son Justin, this woman began to cry with tears of joy and blessings; naturally all the other women began crying, all the men were looking at each other with this puzzled, "What's up with all this?" face.

Justin's teachers would always ask me, "Where did you get this kid? He's so good and sweet."

I replied, "Don't you remember two years earlier you had my other son?"

Same house, same rules, same parents, different children. God is just so wonderful. He is our creator.

The Black Stallion

When Nick was about ten or eleven years old, I remember one day when I came home, he was in his room, and he had had a rough day—discipline from the time he woke up to the time he went to bed. He was crying one of those deep, deep cries. I sat down next to him, and said, "What's wrong?"

"Dad, I'm so bad."

At this point, I'm starting to get emotional too. "What do you mean, you're so bad?"

"I get so many disciplines compared to Justin. I'm so bad."

I just sat there, thinking, "God, help me out here."

I wanted to say, "You're right." But God quickened my mind and rescued me. Just a few nights earlier, we had watched the movie *The Black Stallion.* So instead, I said, "Nicholas, remember that horse in the movie? They couldn't put that horse behind a normal fence, could they? A four-foot fence was nothing; he'd just jump it. That horse was a black stallion and he was strong-willed; God made it that way. Nick, you're just like the Black Stallion. Yes, you're harder to train, Son. Yes, you need more discipline, but think of it as just needing taller fences. I know it's hard on both you and us sometimes, but you are worth it, and God gave you a gift. Your strength and your strong will are a gift from God, and someday you are going to use that strong will to do great things for God."

After we had already named Nicholas, we found out that the name means "a leader of people." These strong-willed kids are the Peters and Pauls. I praise the Lord for Nick's strong will. Parents ask me all the time, "Does Nick let you say these things?"

"Are you kidding, Nick's a star! He'll ask you, 'Want me to sign your book?'" Nick is so confident in who he is in Christ. He is a tool for the Lord, and God was using him in my life to help transform me into the image of Christ.

I never had to go to school and have a meeting with Justin's teachers. I never had to set up a discipline for Justin for bad behavior when he came home from school. I never had to set a homework time for Justin. But with Nick, I had to do those things. He was different. He needed the structure, because without it, he ran amuck. He needed us to come alongside him to help him in these areas.

Be willing to come alongside your children, without comparing them to their sisters or brothers. They are different. If God has blessed you with a strong-willed child, do not look upon it as a genetic dysfunction; praise God for him or her.

Use these tools and you will see God bring about transformation. Failures and mistakes are common; they are our opportunity to train them. Do not take their mistakes personally or forget that it is your job to train your children. It is hard work, but do not give up.

Would you intentionally rebel against God? Would you tell Him, "I don't accept Your plan"? You may not tell Him verbally, but you tell Him by your actions. If God has blessed you with a strong-willed child, be willing to engage and stay consistent and give the extra time and energy it takes. When you get angry and yell or give up and relinquish your responsibility, you are telling God, "I don't trust You; You made a mistake; You gave me a task that is beyond Your ability to help me do it correctly," and that is a very serious accusation to make.

---

[1] Survey of State Prison Inmates, 1991, U.S. Department of Justice, Bureau of Justice Statistics Special Report, August 1995

CHAPTER TWELVE

Train Behaviors—
Not Attitudes

As parents, we have probably all experienced the "attitude," as in: "Don't you give me that attitude, young lady!" Unfortunately, it is very easy to confuse bad attitudes with wrong behaviors; but they are not the same, and they must be dealt with differently.

This is a big issue, more so for women than for men, because God created women to be more emotional. When negative attitudes arise, the temptation for Mom is to follow the child around the house, pleading, "What's wrong with you?" When the child does not respond with the appropriate change in attitude, the situation can escalate to an argument.

Attitude is "a posture or position; a feeling, opinion or mood[1]." *Behavior,* on the other hand, is "the act or manner of behaving[2]." In other words, behavior is something that is done or not done, ie, breaking a rule or not doing what is expected.

God gave each of us emotions from joy to anger, excitement to boredom. And each of us experiences different emotions in response to the situations around us. Although our behavior is often tied to our emotional state, or attitude, there is a distinct difference. We cannot choose our emotions, but we can adjust our behavior. Children learn to adjust their behavior through loving discipline.

Let me explain the difference between attitude and behavior. Psalm 4:4 tells us, "Be angry, and do not sin." Anger is the attitude; the bad behavior is an action. Your response to a bad attitude is simply to tell your child, "You can be sad or mad but you may not kick the wall because that is a behavior. You can be mad as all get out but because God says I'm the authority and this is the rule of the house, you'd better not let something disrespectful come out of your mouth, allowing your negative attitude to manifest into a wrong action that will result in you receiving the predetermined discipline."

Attitudes, unlike behaviors, stem from the heart and the heart is not changed through the disciplining process. The heart of a child can only be changed through their willingness to accept their parents' authority and to receive, through them, God's love and instructions as they disciple them.

It is important to understand that a rebellious heart is a miserable heart. A child with a rebellious heart has no peace, no joy, no contentment, and no lasting pleasure—all by God's perfect design. What more can a parent add to that? We must learn that we cannot control our children's attitudes and emotions, any more than we can control our own. Attempting to discipline a child for a bad attitude is a losing battle, it's controlling and can provoke them to wrath. Instead, we must allow them to feel the way they feel without getting drawn into something we will regret later.

As a parent, if you know that your child is harboring bitterness toward you or is rebelling against God's plan for their life, your response must be prayer and patience without compromise. Do not compromise by allowing your child's bad attitude make you angry or resentful or to misrepresent God in the way you treat him or her. Do not allow their bad attitude to rob you of your inner peace or to dictate how you follow through with your agreed method of discipline or discipleship.

Don't Be Manipulated

In many cases, kids, especially teens, use attitude as a form of manipulation and/or revenge. The word *manipulation* means "to control or play upon by artful, unfair and insidious means, especially to one's own advantage[3]."

Children will try to manipulate their parents to not follow through and discipline them, or to change the rules. For example, when parents are aware that their child frequently exhibits a poor attitude for hours after discipline is received, they will sometimes refrain from disciplining, because they do not want to deal with the attitude that comes along with it. But a right response should be, "Let her be miserable and pray for her." But follow through with a discipline if she breaks a rule and the motivator if she refuses the discipline.

Some children will premeditatedly attempt to use attitude for manipulation to guilt their parents into allowing them to do something they would not normally be permitted to do. For example, one sixteen year old girl manipulated her mom into allowing her to go to a concert she knew she was not supposed to attend. The daughter acted sad and depressed every day for a week. As a typical nurturer, her mom asked her daily, "What's wrong?"

All week long, the teen merely sighed, "Oh, Mom. I don't know. I'm just not happy. I don't know why" Finally on Thursday, she said, "Mom, I'm just sad; I don't have any friends." At this point, her mom had been manipulated to the point where she just wanted her poor daughter to be happy. So the young girl said, "If I could just go to this concert tomorrow night with my friends, I would feel better."

"Well, what concert is that?"

When the daughter told her mom which concert, she replied, "Oh, that's not a good concert."

Once again, the young girl sighed, "Oh, Mom . . ."

Her mom replied, "OK, I'll let you go, and I'll tell Dad . . . Oh, never mind; let's not tell him after all. I know he'll get mad. So let's keep this between us." The girl's manipulation had sucked her mom right in!

You must not let manipulating attitudes wear you down.

Do Not Seek Revenge

Revenge means "to inflict injury in return for an insult." Some children know that if they exhibit a bad attitude, their parents will normally become angry themselves. When you become angry, this gives your children satisfaction that is very damaging to his or her character development, as well as to your foundation and authority, but it takes two to play that game. Don't allow your kids to entice you to practice revenge; don't let their attitude or behavior affect your inner peace. Do not show any emotion; stick with your discipline plan. If you won't join in, they will eventually quit playing this unhealthy, childish game. They will soon discover the attitude revenge game is no fun to play alone.

If you are allowing your children to make you angry or upset because of their bad attitude, you are showing them you are not standing on solid ground, that your God is weak. They can simply cop an attitude and you flip out. You exemplify sinful and weak character yourself when they can pull your emotional "strings" and get you to start reacting to them with anger or revenge.

Reacting in the flesh to your child's attitude also erodes your authority. No one wants to follow a weak leader. Anyone who has been in the armed forces understands that if you have a weak "wimp" of a captain, you have no desire to follow him. Children are no different. If a child can control their parents' inner peace and get them angry just by copping an attitude, that reveals weak leadership.

Revenge Versus Training

If your attitude, when disciplining your children, is motivated by a revengeful heart due to their attitude, your children will know it. This is very selfish and immature. When we say things like, "Hey, you do that again, Buster, I'll ruin your life," is that discipline? No. "You won't go anywhere for a month if you try to pull that again." Is that discipline? No, that is revenge. Reacting with revenge distorts the whole plan that you are trying to put into place. Revenge does not train, but causes children to become defiant, and causes division between parents and children, along with eroding your influence prematurely.

If you and your children have been playing this sinful game for a while, it may take some time to break the bad habit, for both of you. Be patient and stay the course, and the Lord will bring victory. Remember, if the bad attitude turns into a poor behavior choice, such as yelling at you, using a bad word, kicking the wall, slamming the door, whatever, then assess the predetermined discipline for that behavior, but do not react to the attitude.

The Lord has instructed us to *train up our children*, not to inflict injury in reaction to their childish and foolish choices. If our thoughts are to get even with them and/or hurt them in some way because they just will not do what we ask, then this is *our* problem, not our children's. The Lord gave us these children and expects us to raise them in the way He desires, even though sometimes it is hard to do. If you have had the wrong motive in the disciplining of your children, repent and ask for forgiveness from both your child and the Lord.

Training our children as the Lord requires means following His plan of discipline. Proper predetermined disciplines relate to the circumstances and train our children. It is fair and not motivated by anger or revenge; it transforms and shapes our children's character towards maturity. Our children must be motivated by love and obedience to God, not selfishness, anger, or the desire to get revenge. Giving children things that they hate to do is revenge, not training. For example: forcing your son to write: "I will not argue" five hundred times, simply because he dislikes doing it, is not training, it is revenge.

Similarly, many parents think, "My daughter's phone is her lifeline, so if I threaten to take it away every time she does something wrong, she will behave." That is revenge, not training. I'll bring more clarity to this shortly. Hang in there.

Stay the Course

When parents see their children rolling their eyes, pouting, refusing to talk, wanting to stay in their room, doing all their artful, insidious, selfish, childish tricks, they must not engage; stick to the training plan.

When I was a child, I used to hold my breath when I did not get my way. Eventually I would turn purple, and my mother would finally give in to my demands. At some point, my mother consulted a pediatrician. He told her, "Don't do anything" in response to my attitude.

My mom worried, "What if he passes out?"

The doctor said, "Let him."

A couple of days later, we came home from church with our good Sunday school clothes on. My brothers went running down the street, and I wanted to run too. But my mother said, "No, Craig, go change your clothes." Of course, I started to hold my breath. My mother just stood there by the car, watching me. Pretty soon I started turning purple and started wobbling. I looked down, and one foot was on the concrete, and one foot was on the grass. My mother could see that my brain was trying to figure it out, which way should I fall? But before my brain could figure that out, I passed out, and hit my head hard on the ground. I never held my breath again.

When your child is throwing a fit and flip-flopping on the floor, casually ask him, "Does that make you feel better?"

If he kicks the walls, remind him, "Don't kick my walls, don't scream, and don't say something mean."

"I hate you, Mom!"

"Oh, poor choice. I understand you're upset, Honey, I know you are. Remember, that's disrespect. Here is your consequence (the predetermined discipline)."

Let your children go through their motions. When they know that you are not bothered by them, guess what? When you are not serving the ball back, they will eventually quit.

I once had a thirteen-year-old girl in my office throwing fits like a three-year-old, and her parents just said, "You don't understand how hard she is, she throws fits all the time when she does not get her way"

The girl obviously knew her behavior greatly bothered her mother. The mind games and manipulation had gone on for years, and her mom's reaction had trained her to continue to act like a baby even as a teenager. Her father had never stepped up to make her stop either. He should have told his wife long ago, "Honey, please be quiet and let me handle it from here. You're out of the picture on this." The girl had been *taught* to be this way by her parents' reluctance to work at stopping her, and giving in to her wishes and not disciplining her to correct her poor behavior.

When women are unwilling to listen to their husbands and yield to their authority, when it's time to disengage from the child who is acting out in this way, the mother's verbal engaging can be ruining their relationships and lowering themselves down to the child's level. Children are able to engage their parents because their parents are willing to argue and debate.

There were times I have walked in while a conversation was going on between my wife and my son, and it was escalating, but she did not recognize it. I said to my son, "Remember who you're talking to. She's my wife. She's my queen. You don't use that tone of voice, ever."

My wife did not even see it; she was too engaged in the conversation. I would tell Nick to go do a discipline, *now!* Later, my wife and I would discuss how they got to that point. She would say, "Well, he said this, then I said this, and it just seemed to escalate."

"Honey, OK, way back here, you should have said, 'That's the end of this discussion.' Way back here. 'That's the end of it. Nick, I heard your side of it, that's enough. I don't want to discuss it anymore. If you open your mouth one more time in regards to this discussion, you will get a discipline. I'm not going to engage you and continue in this conversation for you to try to change my mind.'"

That is how I helped my wife. I reminded her, "Don't engage. Don't let his emotions grab you; don't buy into his attitude."

Parents, work together as a team to train up your children. Pray, do not compromise, do not engage, and you will have success.

[1] *Webster's New International Dictionary of the English Language; Second Edition Unabridged*; G & C Merriam Company, Publishers, Springfield, MA 1944

[2] *Webster's New International Dictionary of the English Language; Second Edition Unabridged*; G & C Merriam Company, Publishers, Springfield, MA 1944

[3] *Webster's New International Dictionary of the English Language; Second Edition Unabridged*; G & C Merriam Company, Publishers, Springfield, MA 1944

Chapter Thirteen

Practical Tools for Training

For Toddlers

Before we begin looking at practical implementation of the four tools of training, I want to explain the ten "Toddler Property Laws" for those of you who are blessed with children age eighteen months to four-years old:

1. If I like it, it is mine.
2. If it is in my hands, it is mine.
3. If I can take it from you, it is mine.
4. If I had it a week ago, it is mine.
5. If it is mine, it must never appear to be yours in any way.
6. If I am doing or building something, all the pieces are mine.
7. If it looks just like mine, it is mine.
8. If I think it is mine, it is mine.
9. If it is near me, it is mine.
10. If it is broccoli, it is yours.

When our little beauties come home from the hospital, they are absolutely self-consumed; and, as we know, sharing does not come naturally. So let's look at some things that we can do during these toddler years, most commonly known as the "terrible twos." This is the age when your kids are spilling things, throwing things, often hurting themselves, and doing embarrassing things. Testing you in every area is also very common; trying to keep a sense of humor during this time, in order to keep from losing your mind, is very important.

During the first five years, establishing your authority and instilling boundaries are critical. Children at this age will challenge your parental authority daily. Do not panic.

When my son, Nicholas, was between three and four years old, I got a phone call at work from my wife. She was so upset; she was crying and I was trying to figure out what had happened. Finally she told me the story. She had been at the grocery store. She had put Justin in the cart, but Nick was walking beside her when he had found the toy section. So he brought some toy over and said, "Mommy, I want this."

My wife said, "No, put it back" and kept walking. She got to the end of the aisle, turned around, and saw that Nick was not following. So she said, "Nick, come on." He started walking the other way. So she left Justin there in the basket, and started going after Nick.

She got halfway down the aisle, and Nick started running away. Now she had a crisis on her hands. She had a little two-year old in the basket at one end of the aisle, and a four-year old starting to run the other way. So she went back and got the cart, but she was really starting to panic. She began chasing Nick around the store with this cart full of groceries. He stayed just out of her reach, so that she could not catch him. Finally she made a mad dash, grabbed him, went back, grabbed Justin, and left the store in tears, leaving all the stuff in the basket.

Once I had heard the story, I got in the car, drove home, spanked Nick and threatened his life (this was before I understood these principles I am sharing with you). I said, "Don't you ever do this again!" and I went back to work.

Less than a week later, the phone rang at work again, and it was my wife, sobbing so hard. I thought someone had died.

"What, Honey, what?"

"He did it again."

"Did what again?"

She said, "In the store!"

I came home, I went into his room, and I gave him a licking you would think he would never forget. I came out, and my wife was still crying, still upset, sobbing, "I can't do this anymore."

I said, "Honey, look, you'll never shop with him again, I promise. You'll wait until I come home, or I'll go to the grocery store. You won't have to do it, I promise you. I won't put you through this again."

I went in and told him, "Nick, you're not going with Mom anymore to the grocery store. Either I'm going to do it, or you're going to stay home."

A couple of weeks went by, and my wife needed some milk and bread, and I happened to be home. She said, "Would you go down and get some?"

Nick piped up, "Hey, Dad, can I go with you?"

"Sure." I did not think, in my wildest dreams, this little four-year old, who was all of forty pounds, would challenge *my* authority in the store. On the way to the store, I looked at Nick and said, "Nick, you know the rules?"

"Yes, Dad."

So I got the milk and bread, and I went to stand in the express line, ready to check out. But I looked around, and Nick was not behind me. He was standing about thirty feet away, with a toy in his hands. I said, "Nick, put it back." But he did not move. He just put his head down.

What started coming over me at that point was definitely demonic! The milk carton was ready to pop in my hands. The guy behind me started backing up, everyone began to notice what was going down, but I did not even care. I was oblivious to the people around me; I was looking at Nick, thinking, "How dare you?"

"Nick, do it NOW!" Still, he did not listen. Then I said something that I pray none of you will ever say. I said, "Nick, if you don't do it now, I'm going to drop-kick you across the store. I don't care who's here." Finally he darted off and put the toy away.

We got into the car, and I spanked him. We got home and I spanked him again. It was many situations like this that caused my wife and me to begin to pray and look for help in dealing with Nick. I knew what I was doing was not right, and the spankings did not seem to help. This was a time before I learned how to properly deal with disciplining Nick.

You parents, who are blessed with a strong-willed child like this, hang in there. The tools you are going to learn really do work.

Dad's—Get Involved

It is important, Dads, when you have younger kids, that you are involved. We need to work together when our children are small. When I first got into lay ministry, I was doing both the pre-marriage counseling at our church. And when you are involved in the ministry, it is important that you get to church on time. It was very embarrassing for me to walk in late.

We lived about a twenty-minute drive from church. One Sunday morning I was driving about ninety-five miles an hour down the freeway, and my wife looked over at me and said, "Why are you speeding? You should slow down!"

I said, "If you wouldn't make us so late, I wouldn't have to speed!"

She could tell I was a little agitated. There was silence for a few moments; then she calmly said, "Why don't you help me in the morning?"

That had never crossed my mind. I looked at her and said, "What do you mean, help? I get up; I get the cereal bowls out. Once in a while I even put the cereal in the bowls before the kids come to breakfast. I even make the coffee. What else do you want me to do?" I was completely oblivious.

She said, "Why don't you get the kids dressed?"

At this point, I had a crisis going on in my head. "Do I take this on or what?" I said, "OK, fine. Starting next week, it's mine."

The next week rolled around, and I got up that morning, knowing I was going to prove her wrong. The kids were going to be dressed and we were going to be *on time*. I walked into the boys' room, "Hey, come on boys, let's get going; come on." I went downstairs, got everything all ready. But I did not hear anything upstairs; it was silent.

So I walked back into their room, and these two little boys were still in bed! "Get up, right now!" I pulled their sheets down. "Get out or I'm going to spank you!" Pretty soon they were upset and crying, and I was shoving their clothes on.

A side note about strong-willed kids: when possible, give them a choice. Nicholas always thought he had to be in control. I eventually learned to pull two pairs of Levis out for him to choose from. I could not even tell the difference between the two pairs, but that made him feel like he had a little bit of control. Sometimes you can just give them a choice in a small area, and it makes things work smoother. Justin did not care if you put a pink shirt on him with green pants.

Back to the first "dress rehearsal" morning. I thought I had won, but I was wrong. We got into the car on time, and as we drove down the road I was feeling pretty good. I looked over at my wife, and her expression said it all. She was looking at me with that face that said, "You big idiot."

I said, "Hey, we're on time."

She replied, "Yeah, but look in the back." Both of the boys were back there, red-eyed, tears running down. Sure they were ready to go to church and praise God!

As my wife and I discussed how I could do better, I learned how to put a sock on my hand, make a little puppet and go up under the sheets, "Hello, good morning!" Or I would do the old "Wet Willy" in the ear. I would lie next to them and tell a story (I used to tell these dumb dog stories about this dog that would chase cats up a tree and not know how to get down, putting his head in a bottle, etc; I would make them up as I went along). I made wake-up time a fun time.

I learned that if I just got their motors running in the morning, their minds thinking, for ten or fifteen minutes, then when I said, "OK, come on, let's get ready to go," they were much better about getting ready and getting going with a cooperating spirit. I learned to adapt without compromise. Did it take time? Yes. But this was my job until my children were able to do it on their own.

So Dads, you can engage here and help. It is not "your part and my part"; it is "our part."

Practical Points for Little Ones

There are some practices which are especially important when you have small children: love them, do not yell or get angry. Stay calm—if you lose control, you lose credibility. It is critical to teach them to obey and respect your authority those first five years. Be consistent—if you say you are going to do something, then follow through.

If possible, try to kid-proof rather than continue an ongoing battle. Let me explain: if you have a strong-willed child who keeps getting into your older kid's toys, which are stored down low, and every day it is a big fight because your three-year old just cannot wait to go in there and play with those toys, and never puts them away or breaks them, you might want to build a shelf and put them up higher. We do not think twice about locking up the poison, but it can be just as important to lock up those "bones of contention."

When you are disciplining your children, you need to do it in love. When you are disciplining your younger kids, especially if they are forcing you to bring forth a motivator, they may look at you and say, "You don't love me, you just spanked me."

Explain to them, "no, this is another form of love. God says love is discipline which includes punishment, and if you refuse a predetermined discipline, I need to find some way to motivate you." But of course, if you have an angry face and are yelling, there is no way you are going to convince them you are loving them at this moment. You must remove those things from your training practices completely.

Sample Rules

You need to establish some real boundaries by the time your children hit fifteen to eighteen months. *See Appendix A for Sample Rules And Disciplines for children 18 months through 5 years old.*

Respect – Obey Parents

First, from the time they can walk to the time they leave your house, the number one rule must be that they respect you. Remember, in those first five years, when you are teaching them this rule, you are also defining what respect is. Obviously a three-year old does not know what the word "respect" means. When they get mad and say, "I hate you," they do not understand that was disrespectful, the first time. So when things come up and they respond in the wrong way, you need to say, "Now look, I understand you're upset, but what you just said was disrespectful. So the next time you say that, you will have a conse- quence — a discipline — for disrespect."

Not obeying your command is also a form of disrespect. If you ask your child to come here, stop doing that, get away from that, etc…, and they do not comply, you need to discipline them. Do not get into the habit of raising your voice or using their middle name to get their attention more sternly. If they do not comply, just follow through and give them the predetermined discipline.

A typical discipline for disrespect would be a time out. I recommend that whatever age your child is, that is the length of time you use: if they are three, they sit for three minutes. Use the playpen for little kids, so they are not able to crawl out. They will understand the concept: when you say, "No," and they continue doing it, you pick them up, put them in the playpen, and set the timer.

Now, with some of your strong-willed children, those who are three-, four-, five-years old, who are more strong-willed, you need to define what "sit in the chair" means. If you do not define it, they will soon be standing on the chair or scooting it across the floor. When you set them down on the chair, their mind is thinking, "I've got to win here. I'm not in control. I don't like this."

So you have to define it for them, "Butt on the chair, chair in the same spot."

Your more compliant children will just sit there.

I do not suggest putting the chair in the corner; just put them at the dinner table, or in Dad's easy chair. The idea is not to make them wear a dunce cap in the corner, but to subject them to your authority and discipline.

When was the last time God made you stand in the corner with your nose against the wall for your disobedience? God does not do that to us; we should not do it to our children. Foolishness is not bad; they just need to be trained "discipline." If they get out of the chair before the timer is done, they are asking for the motivator—punishment. If you are using spanking as your punishment, just spank them and put them back in the chair and start the time over.

Bedtime

There is no biblical instruction for when your children should stop falling asleep in your bed. I have heard some people try to find scriptural grounds to say that having your kids fall asleep in your bed will cause emotional damage. Now *that* is foolish. There is nothing wrong with allowing your kids to fall asleep in your bed, but there may be some possible difficulty when you begin to break this habit.

With my boys, I told my wife, "That is never happening." There were times when they were scared and we would allow them to, but it was not very common. With my little girl, it was different. She was our little princess: both my wife and I let it happen often. My wife finally said, "Honey, I think it's time for her to learn to fall asleep in her own bed." I do suggest by the time they are three-years old you should begin to train them to fall asleep in their own beds.

I had a husband and wife come in for marriage counseling that had a thirteen-year old that was still sleeping in their bed. Obviously the husband was very unhappy about this. This woman had been physically abused by her stepdad when she was in bed, and was full of so much fear and unforgiveness that she allowed her son to fall asleep in her bed since he was born. That is wrong and very unhealthy for everyone: the son, and the parents' marriage. It was a very difficult time breaking both the son's bad habit and his mother's emotional fears, but they found victory through forgiveness and a good plan.

If you have a husband, it is good, if possible, for moms to let dads lead in putting the children to bed. Moms will just end up lying down and falling asleep with the kids, leaving the husband to go to sleep by himself. Men, you need to step up to the plate if need be. If the child has been falling asleep in your bed, they are not always excited to stop doing it.

It is good to tie the transition to a birthday. Dad should tell the child: "OK, you're three, you know what that means? It is time for you to start sleeping in your own bed."

"I don't want to, I like falling asleep in your bed."

"I understand that, Honey, but it's now time; 8:30 is your bedtime. Here's your water. Here's a night-light. I'll pray with you and leave the door open."

"I want Mommy."

"No, you already said goodnight to Mommy." For the next five days you may want to lie down with them or kneel next to their beds for ten or fifteen minutes to help the transition, but you need to work toward training them in this. You explain to them, "If you get out of your bed, it will be a swat on your butt (a rare exception to the rule) and back to bed." You comfort them for just a few moments, and you walk out of the room.

Usually when you walk out, they will begin to cry. Set a timer for five minutes. After five minutes, go back in there and comfort them (again, just for a few moments): "I'm here, we didn't leave you."

"Where's Mom, did she leave?"

"No, she's here, but it is time for bed now."

"I want to see her."

"No."

"I want Mom."

"No, Dad's here." You explain that you know this is hard but it is part of growing up. You encourage them; you may consider rubbing, scratching, or tick-ling their back a little bit, but then you get up and leave. After you leave the room a second time you set the timer for ten minutes, and you do not go back into the room until that ten minutes is up, unless they get out of bed. If they do, you follow through, one swat, put them to bed, and walk back out again. Stay consistent with this. Every time you do it, add another five minutes to the timer. Usually in three to four days, the transition is complete.

Bedtime was a difficult time for my son Nicholas. He just didn't want to fall asleep; he thought he was going to miss something. He was just one of those special children. He would purposely wedge himself in the corner of his bed so he could not get comfortable. He knew if he would lay flat, he would fall asleep. Several times a week, there were nights that he would cry for over two hours before falling asleep.

He would cry until his little eyeballs would swell up into little slits. My wife and I would lie in bed thinking, "We should invent some kind of smelling stuff to knock him out; we would be millionaires — because there *has* to be other kids like Nick!"

It was very hard on both of us! A few times when I went out of town, my wife got suckered into letting him fall asleep in our bed for the nights I was gone. We had at least two more nights of struggle to get it back in order after I came home.

With Justin, we said, "Hey, Justin, this is the bedtime."

"OK." That was it.

In my family, we have a bunch of kids between us. All together, my parents have a total of thirty-nine grandkids, and thirty-four live in San Diego. We have a great time together! My youngest brother and his family moved to North Carolina a few years ago.

When my kids were young, we would all go camping together. The sun would rise at 6:00 am, and there Nick was at five-years old, wide awake. Everyone else was asleep, but he would be demanding, "Get me dressed." He would go out walking around, knocking on everyone's camper doors.

Then at 10:00 at night, he would still be out there by the fire when all the other kids were crashed out asleep, but he would be saying, "What's next?" He was a special boy (*and you thought you had the only strong-willed, hyper child*).

Mom . . . You're Not a Maid

Another rule should be: "Pick up your own messes." Moms, you are not maids. You can start doing this with their toys at a young age. Obviously most three-year olds are not going to patiently sit there and pick up their toys; it is OK to sit down and help them. But if they do not help you, the discipline is that you confiscate the toy (make sure they see you), put it in a brown bag, go to a closet, and put it up. Say, "The discipline for not helping Mommy is that your toy stays there for the next two days."

My son Justin would just forget about that toy. Nick, on the other hand—guess which toy he wanted for the next two days? That one. Good discipline relates to the situation.

No Means No

"No means no." That can be a rule. Give them a discipline for asking over and over after you have already said "no." Another rule typical for small kids is "no whining." Whining oftentimes is simply manipulation. Give them a time-out each time.

Exceptions to the Spanking Rules

Now in some cases, such as at bedtime or on Sunday morning when it is almost time to leave for church and the kids are in the bathtub, you cannot give a discipline like a time out for not getting out of the bath when you say. Instead, you can say to them, "Listen, I want you out of the tub now. If you do not get out of the tub now, you're going to get a spanking." That is the exception, though, not the rule. There are times when you do not have a choice in the matter; you have to say, "Here's the rule, here's the motivator. Respond correctly, or I will follow through." This is used only in time-constraint situations.

Principles of Spanking

#1—Plan Ahead

Choose ahead of time what will be corrected with spanking (Prov. 6:16-19). Most parents go directly from the broken rule to the punishment. That does not work. You must go to the predetermined discipline first, and if they refuse the predetermined discipline, then you go to punishment. It is important that you know beforehand how and when and for what you are going to issue punishment, so that it is not based upon your emotions at the time.

#2 — Use Love

Spank in love. For a punishment to be effective, it must be done in the context of a loving relationship. What that means is no angry yelling and screaming. It is absolutely fine to spank your child without smiling; you can be firm, without twisting your face in anger.

#3 — Find Privacy

Spank your child in private, away from the other brothers and sisters or other adults.

Think about this: let's say you are on your way to church, and right down the street from the church, you get pulled over by the police for speeding. You are sitting there on the side of the road, and everyone you know is driving by on their way to church. Would you get out of your car and call out, "Hey, I'll be there in a minute. Save a place for me!" No, of course not. You would be saying, "Come on officer; please hurry. Everyone's going by, somebody might see me," all the while hiding your face. It is embarrassing—and we are adults. Do you think it is any less embarrassing to your children? No, it is not.

When you are at someone's house, or in a public setting, find somewhere private. Many people in our society believe that spanking is illegal. It is not. Spanking your children correctly is still legal. But, if you spank in public, there is a chance that social services could show up at your door to interview you and your kids. They may even try to remove your children from your home. I have worked with cases like this when they did remove one of the children for this reason. In some cases it went on for several months in court. If the spanking was done correctly, the judge would merely assign counseling and return the child to their home, because there is no law against spanking. But because of the many parents who have done it wrong and in anger, you must be wise here.

#4—Be Consistent

Be consistent. If you say you are going to spank your child for certain punishment, make sure that you always follow through.

#5—Explain

Talk with your child in a firm but loving voice, and explain why the punishment is taking place. "I'm spanking you, Honey, because you're refusing to sit in the chair. If you would have sat in the chair and accepted the discipline, then we wouldn't have to go through this."

#6—Affirm Your Love

Affirm your love after punishing your child. Hug him—but only if he wants to be hugged. Be open and willing to affirm your love in the way he/she is open to receive it.

The last thing Nick wanted to do after he was punished or even disciplined was to be hugged. He would wait about half an hour, and then he would just come and jump on my back and want to wrestle. Justin, on the other hand, immediately wanted someone to hug him. He wanted to be reassured right away, and he is a hugger. So is Katie.

Each child is different. If one does not want to hug for a while, then do not hug them.

#7—Make It Immediate

Spank your child as soon as possible after the act of defiance, and use the opportunity to motivate your child to accept your training. Now, sometimes that is not possible. You may be in public, or you may be at someone's house, where there is not a room that you can go into. So in those situations you have to say, "Honey, sit right here until we go home. You know what's going to happen." If he does not listen, in some cases you may have to leave and deal with this.

#8—Never in Anger

Never spank in anger or when you are not in control of your own emotions.

#9—Show Respect

Never spank a child in a way that shows disrespect. Some parents make their children pull their pants down and lay over a chair. Obviously, most kids are not going to turn around and say, "OK, spank me." Nick was like a rabbit. I hooked my hand right up underneath his armpit and backed him up against the bed so that he would not spin doughnuts around me.

The right place to spank is on the buttocks, in the fatty area. If you stay within that butt area, you are also on safe ground with the court systems. You move out of that area, you are crossing some lines.

#10—Use the Right Amount

Never spank more than necessary; use a measured amount of pain. Determine ahead of time how many swats they are going to get. Do not worry if they say, "That didn't hurt." It is not that you are trying to make them cry. If it is two swats, that is what it is, no matter what.

What you can do is if they say, "That didn't hurt" is say, "OK, I'm going to ask you a question, and you're going to have five seconds to answer. Now let me show you how long five seconds is: one, two, three, four, five. That's how long you have to answer this question. If you don't answer or if you answer incorrectly, you're going to get another two swats. Here is the question: do you want another spanking?"

Now they have a crisis. If they say, "No," that means the first one really did hurt. If they say, "Yes," that would be dumb; they are asking for another spanking. Most of the time they say nothing at all, until you follow through, and that usually ends the problem of them responding in that way.

#11—Spank for the Right Reason

Never spank a child for childishness or messiness. Spank them for willful defiance, when he or she is unwilling to accept your discipline.

When I was about eight or nine years old, I loved chocolate milk. We had eight kids in our family; you can imagine there were not many desserts around, so chocolate milk was a big thing for us. We must have gone through five gallons of milk a day in our house.

I remember one time, after my parents had just laid new carpet, I was making chocolate milk. Half of the kitchen was carpet, and half was linoleum. I was, of course, on the carpet side, and I spilled the chocolate powder all over the brand new carpet. Now being a dumb ten-year old, I did not know I should get the vacuum. Instead, I went and got a wet rag. And no matter how much I rubbed and scraped, the stain just kept getting bigger and blacker. That is an example of childishness. It was an accident.

When you come home and find your ten-year old has left your tools out in the rain all night, and there is rust on them, think about this: what do you value more, your kid or the tools? Say, "Poor choice, here's your discipline." God knows how to bring these tests that reveal what we value more. Remember, if you blow it, ask for forgiveness.

#12—Deal With Manipulation

Do not allow your child to manipulate you. Many times your child will try to divert the deserved spanking by accusing you of not loving them or by apologizing profusely. But if they did not listen to you and respond to what you have asked them to do with discipline, you must follow through. Do not let them turn this into a temporary power struggle.

#13—Deal With Excessive Crying

Excessive crying, screaming, or yelling during or after spanking must be dealt with. What can you do when your child is screaming like you are killing them? Here is a way you can break the cycle. Let them know if they act this way, they will also be put into their room for a period of time. Follow through with the spanking. Then if they are doing this behavior again, put them in their room, and say, "When you quit screaming or crying, I will start the timer. (Again, you can use their age for the amount of time they are to be in their room after they have calmed down.) If you come out of the room before that timer goes off, you will get another spanking, and go back in your room."

Once they figure out that you are going to stay calm and consistent, what eventually will happen is you will hear their little voice, "I'm not crying now."

"I know. I started the timer, Honey."

"Is it done yet?"

"No, I'll let you know."

The Paddle or the Hand?

Worldly psychology has taught for many years "don't use your hand—you need to separate yourself from the spanking." But do you really think when you are spanking your child with an object that he does not know who is swinging it?

Personally, I am a firm believer in using your hand. When God speaks of "the rod of correction," He is speaking of the tool of measurement and the authority. He does not expect you to grab a stick and beat your child.

I encourage you to use your hand. With your hand, you have full control of how hard you spank, and you can measure how much pain you dole out. With your hand, you can also control where you are spanking more effectively.

God uses the term "hand of correction" over and over again throughout Scripture. When you use your hand, the same hand that rubs their face, that holds them, that feeds them and loves them is the same hand that corrects them.

So, if you are going to use any object at all, throw the spoon away, and get a flat paddle. If you use a spoon, and you hit too far down, leaving a bruise, you are opening the door for possible abuse accusations.

I have counseled hundreds of kids and hear their responses to what they saw and what they felt when their parent used an object. It was not so much the spanking that bothered them, but the object their parents used. My experience is that your hand is the best tool for spanking. God set the example for us (1 Sam. 5:11, 2 Chron. 30:12, Job 19:21, Eccles. 2:24, 26 amplified).

The same hand that blesses us also punishes us.

When Dad's Not Home

What happens during the day when Dad's not home and the kids need a discipline? Simple:

"Help me pick up these toys."

"No, I don't want to."

"Well, this is one of the rules Dad has. If you don't help me, remember what the discipline is, the toy gets picked up and gets put away."

Moms, if you are married, lean upon Dad. You are following Dad's rules. Lean upon his authority. Your greatest companionship need as a wife is loving security, so let your husband protect you here. Don't argue with your kids over why a rule exists or a discipline is being given. Just say, "If you have any questions, take it up with Dad."

While There Is Still Hope . . .

"Chasten your son while there is hope, and do not set your heart on his destruction" (Prov. 19:18). The command here is to discipline your children; it is also a warning against parental passivity. A child guilty of wrongdoing should be chastened (disciplined) in the early years while there is still hope. To neglect needed discipline may contribute to even capital punishment under the law later in life.

The Myth of Positive Reinforcement

Our society has embraced the "positive reinforcement" concept of parenting; sadly, most of it is just so wrong and distorted. Using charts and rewards seems to work well with compliant children, but has some serious side effects. Have you noticed how many teens and young adults have this entitlement mentality? Someone owes them everything, and if the reward does not seem good enough, they will just quit! Our culture is infected by this today. This type of parenting does not work, especially with strong-willed kids.

Love is the most powerful motivator, and the most powerful way to build self-worth, not gifts and gimmicks. As we learned in a previous chapter, we are to praise our children because they are a gift from God and daily practice our love for them. Good behavior is expected, not rewarded (Luke 17:7-9). Our love toward them should not change because of their failures: be they a compliant child or a strong-willed child.

Remember when your children began to walk? You helped them and encouraged them as they took their first steps. You did not say, "You're embarrassing me! Get up! I was running by the time I was your age." When they fell, you picked them back up again and continued to help them. God says we must maintain that same type of attitude toward discipline. If we do, that is the best self-worth builder available, not gifts and gimmicks.

In certain situations, however, it is OK for you to put a carrot out there to encourage a particular behavior. For example, my son Nicholas struggled academically. He could read a sentence five times without understanding it. It is a learning problem that I have, my dad had, and seven out of thirty-nine grandkids have been diagnosed with.

Nick would spend hours of work towards his spelling words all week and get a C on his test, while Justin would look them over for fifteen minutes and get an A. It seemed really unfair for Nick. So I would say, "Nicholas, I know this is hard for you, but if you do well, if you work hard on this thing, we're going to do this for you." If I did something like that, I would make sure I took Justin aside, and say, "Look, Justin, I'm going to do this for Nick, because you know how he struggles academically." Then I would make sure I did something for Justin also. In those cases, positive reinforcement is OK.

The Discipline Box

I want to share with you a wonderful little tool called the discipline box, which takes the place of time outs for your older children in most situations. This should be introduced when your children are around the ages of six and older. It can be a jar, or a shoe box or any type of container that you can get into easily. In the box, you place little pieces of paper on which are written chores that are age-appropriate. So if you have a six and an eight-year-old, they could use the same box. Chores like: dust a certain room, vacuum the living room, clean a mirror, sweep the back patio, etc. You fold the papers up and put them in the box. When a rule is broken, let's say disrespect, the new consequence is the discipline box.

Have your kids help put it together. It is so fun when they sit down and help you think up the disciplines to put on those pieces of paper. They are not thinking about themselves getting the disciplines; they are thinking about their brother or sister getting them. They can be pretty vicious and creative about what they say.

When it is time for a discipline, you grab the box, they reach in, and completely at random they pull out a piece of paper and do whatever it says, right then. You can intercede if someone just pulled that one and completed the task; you can have them pull another one.

What happens if they say, "I'm not going to do the discipline"? You motivate them. If, after you spank them, they still do not accept the discipline, they go in their room and they sit there until they are ready to come out and do the discipline. Do not let them out of that discipline. Remember, punishment is not the trainer; it does not educate or build character—discipline does. Follow through with the punishment, but they must finish the discipline also.

Once, when Nick was around eleven-years old, he pulled from the discipline box, which he did often, and the discipline he got said, "Clean all the toilets." The house we had at the time had four bathrooms. My wife and I looked at each other, and said, "Clean the toilets? We don't remember putting that in there." But my wife grabbed her big rubber gloves and the toilet brush, marched him into the bathroom, started showing him how to do the first one, and he was off and running.

While she was gone, I took a look in the box. When she came back into the kitchen, I told her, "Look, there are twice as many as there used to be." So we dumped them out and started going through them. There were some hard ones in there!

Eventually we came across one that said, "Do all of Justin's chores." You see, two days earlier, Nick had been bothering Justin, and Justin wanted to get back at him. So he spiced up the discipline box. Justin would get a discipline, on average, every fourth day; Nick, on the other hand, would sometimes get ten a day. It was his best way to get back at Nick.

We did not discipline Justin for that, not at all. Actually, we thought it was quite funny. As a matter of fact, half the ones he put in there, we left in there. He was very creative.

But I encourage you, put the box up high. When you first implement this, things may happen to that box. If it does not disappear altogether, all the hard things that were written on those sheets of paper will disappear.

As They Get Older: Using Related Disciplines

At about eight years old, it is important to introduce related discipline when appropriate. Let me give you an example. Let's say they are eight years old and they have a bicycle. You live on the dead-end street, which is a fine place to ride. But when you go off that dead-end street, it is too dangerous. So you say to your son, "OK, you can ride all you want right here, but if you cross that line, past that telephone pole, without getting permission from Mom or me, you will lose the privilege of that bike for a week. So choose wisely."

You can be creative here, but make sure it is related. Do not say, "I'm going to take away your game boy." What does that have to do with riding your bike down the street?

Seek the Lord, and ask, "OK, God, what rules do we need for the kids that You gave us?". *See Appendix*

B for Sample Rules and Disciplines for children ages 6 and older.

No Fighting

One of the rules I want to cover here is no fighting and verbal arguing. When this happens, many times parents become both judge and jury trying to figure it out, who started it, who did what first, and pretty soon you just get mad and yell at them, and no one gets disciplined. If no arguing is part of the rule, when you do not know who started what, you merely walk into the room and say, "Alright, the next one that speaks to the other in the next fifteen minutes will get a discipline." You set the timer, and separate them in different areas in the house.

When one of them runs in and says, "He stuck his tongue out at me," you say, "You go do a discipline, because you shouldn't have been looking at him." Then you go get the other one and give him a discipline too. Don't let their childish foolishness control you.

No Lying

A "no lying" rule is a good one. Tell them if they get caught lying, they have double discipline. Then simply give them two disciplines from the list.

Clean Your Own Mess

The rule is clean up your own messes. You walk in the house, you see a mess, and you go tell him, "Clean that up. When you're done, go do a discipline. Remember, I'm not your maid."

One of our rules was "clean up and keep your own bedroom clean." We had them make their beds and straighten their bedrooms before they went to school, but if your own room is not cleaned up, then do not expect your kids to do it either. The first time we made this rule my kids said, "We're not going to have time to pick everything up and make the bed."

"That's right, that's why you should have your bedroom picked up before you go to sleep. So the only thing you have to do in the morning is pull up your sheets." The bedroom is a wonderful training tool.

Sometimes you are going to find a mess, and you are not going to know who made it. If everyone denies it, in some cases, you are not going to figure it out. In that case, just clean it up yourself. Believe me, you will catch them again.

CHAPTER FOURTEEN

Practical Implementation for Adolescents

If the boundaries and foundation of discipline have been well-laid during the first nine years, the transition into adolescence will be a smooth one. Many changes occur between ages thirteen and fifteen. At this point kids are growing physically, rapidly developing their sexuality, and increasing in strength. Emotionally they are becoming more independent. They are much more aware of the opposite sex; they begin to feel a need to be accepted by their peers; and they begin to develop close friendships (see our series called *Understanding Teens*).

When these changes are taking place, they often-times begin to challenge your authority all over again. It is like the "terrible twos" coming back up again, but now they are one hundred pounds heavier. Here are some very important things not to compromise in during this season:

Number one, ***respect toward both parents***. That means no mouthing off and no bossing the other children. I had to discipline Nicholas quite a few times for this, "Nick, we've got two parents in this house; we don't need another one."

Watch out when they start telling you what they are doing, rather than asking.

"I'll be home by 7:00."

In those cases, you need to stop and say, "Whoa, are you asking, or are you telling me?"

"What's the big deal?"

"Well, let me explain. If you're telling me, then no, you're not going any place. If you're asking me, I'll think about it."

It is a power struggle that sneaks up on you. Do not get mad; it is normal, just deal with it consistently.

Number two, the ***morals and values*** that you have established within your home, including your children's personal interests and their pleasures—music, TV, games, etc. Nick was really into music, so in our house we had a rule: you can have any music you want, but if it is not Christian, I had to read and approve the lyrics first. Did we ever catch Nick with inappropriate music? Yes, we did. One time my wife found a bunch of CDs down at the bottom of his drawer. We got on the Internet, looked up those bands, and we could see by the first picture that popped up what they were about. Most of the lyrics were on the Internet as well. So the discipline was the CDs got destroyed, and he had a discipline from the discipline box—one for each CD.

One time seven of the CDs we destroyed were not his; they belonged to his Christian friend. When it got back to the parents that we had destroyed their son's CDs and my son had to do disciplines, they called us, "Oh, we're so sorry, tell your son don't worry about it, he doesn't have to pay him back, because we don't want that in our house either." Then they asked me for advice on how to deal with this out-of-control problem with their son.

Number three, explain to them that *the training can stop when they become responsible adults or when they leave your home*, whichever comes first. Many times kids will say, "Well, I think I don't need to be disciplined anymore."

You just say, "OK, I'll make you a deal. If you stay within the rules, I'll never discipline you again. But, if you break a rule in my house, you are demonstrating to you and me that you need to be disciplined."

Sample Rules

Wake-Up Time

We had a rule about waking up in the morning. If you have a teenage kid and you find yourself going in there two or three times every morning to wake them up, you are not helping that child. Get them an alarm clock. When my boys turned nine years old, I gave them an alarm clock and said, "Wake yourselves up. Get up on your own, get yourselves dressed, get ready for school."

The longer you put this off and don't train them, the harder it becomes when they become teenagers. If they are not ready by a certain time, give them a discipline. The discipline could be "going to bed half an hour or an hour early that night, plus you can do a discipline when you get home." Some teens can be stubborn here. My son Justin got more disciplines for this one than Nick.

Bathroom Schedules

Sharing bathrooms in the morning can be hectic. Give your teens a schedule. "You have from 6:00 to 6:15. At 6:16, you'd better be out of that bathroom. If you're not, you get a discipline." Keep that peace in the home. Fix those areas that may be creating havoc.

Curfew

I want to say this about curfew: one of the worst things you can do is say "curfew is 10:00." When you tell them 10:00 is the curfew, of course they want to be out every night until that time. So they think every plan they make, they have until 10:00. Instead, make it situation specific. Every time they leave your presence, they need to let you know where they are going, who they are going with, which parent is going to be there, who is driving, and when they will be home. If the plans change, they had better call you first and get permission. If they are home at 10:00 one night, 11:00 one night, 8:00 one night, fine, but make that determination as the situation arises, and be careful here: don't let them begin to pull away too soon by being out three or four times each week.

Telephone Privileges

When your kid hits thirteen years old, and the phone is ringing off the hook with all the girls and boys calling, and you never see them anymore because they are in their room, the answer to that problem is not giving them a phone in their room. That is not the answer, because the enemy can use that and have them pull away from you and the family prematurely.

Let me encourage you: having phone and computer chat rules is important, especially with the opposite sex. Set a time frame for what days and the time they can communicate with their friends on the phone or via computer. Also, know who their friends are that they are talking to on the phone. Example: phone or computer chat time is 7:30 to 8:00; the discipline, if the rule is broken is two days no phone or computer. On our website at www.parentingministry we have more suggestions for computer parental controls.

Creative Punishments for Teens

It is a good idea to plan to wean yourself and your children off spanking by the time they are eight to ten years old. Some kids can be weaned off even younger.

Put Them to Work

I have found that work is an effective discipline. When Nick hit twelve to thirteen years old, he began to really challenge my wife's authority again. She would give her discipline, and sometimes he would start to argue with her. By that point, he was too big to spank.

Moms ask me all the time, "When should I stop spanking?"

My reply: "When you can't catch him. When holding him down is becoming a wrestling match, you are past the time to spank."

Teens Challenging Mom's Authority

So what happens then, when Dad is not home, and you give your 110-pound eleven-year old a discipline and he will not do it? At that point, he is in "Shut Down." "Shut Down" means room restriction, no friends, no phone, radio, computer, games, or iPods. Send him to his room until Dad gets home. If he will not go to his room, it's time to call Dad. Dad sits down when he gets home and says, "Son, what was the problem today?"

"Well, I don't think this is fair."

"Really? Go do that discipline now, but for not listening to your mom's authority and going to your room, your punishment you are going to get additional is Saturday work every time; and you will receive one hour's worth of work every time you don't listen to Mom and don't accept going to your room for not doing the predetermined discipline. This is going to be the punishment. When I'm not here, Son, I don't care how big you are, Mom is the authority. I have delegated my responsibility to her when I'm gone. She is doing what I have asked her to do."

Now, I always gave an hour's worth of work. I did not say, "Go work for an hour," or I would have gotten one weed pulled. I would say, "You weed from here to here, and if you're done early for working fast, great; if it takes four hours, or if you take all day, I don't care—your choice, but you will have no freedom until that work is complete."

Nick became a machine. He figured out, "If I work fast and hard, I can work for less than an hour."

Double the Discipline

When my son Nicholas would begin to challenge my wife and not accept the discipline, she would then send him to his room. There was no challenge over that. When I would come home, my wife would tell me what had happened, and I would go in, sit down, and say, "Nick, what happened?" He'd give me his side of the story. "OK, Nick, the reality is, you wanted door number three. We told you that doesn't exist anymore. Go do two disciplines for not doing it when Mom asked you to."

"Shut Down" as a Punishment

On "Shut Down," there is no TV, radio, iPod, no friends, no computer, and no cash flow. Your life consists of school, schoolwork, chores, dinner table, and bathroom. It is used as a punishment if a teen does not accept and do the discipline. If they go do the discipline correctly, their freedom starts again. Many parents use restriction for everything, but it really should only be used in specific instances. It can be used as a related discipline, such as coming home at the wrong time. You told them to be home at 6:00, and they came home at 6:30. "Poor choice, for the next three days, you are on restriction, since you don't have the self-control to choose wisely when you're out of our care."

Restriction should consist of staying home for a designated time frame, no friends over, and no phone privileges during that time, not to be confused with "Shut Down." Remember "Shut Down" is appropriate when a child refuses discipline. At that moment they lose all privileges—they remain in this "Shut Down" until they accept the discipline. If it takes five minutes or five days, what do you care? Act like you have all the time in the world.

They may say to you, "This is ridiculous!"

"I know; I can't believe it either. For something that's going to take you eight minutes, you've been in your room for three days. I can't figure it out, but if that's what you want, that's OK with me."

Creative Disciplines for Teens

My kids grew up with a discipline box, so up until they were in their teens, Nick was still pulling from the box. But when you want to implement a discipline box with your thirteen-year olds, they might think, "What is this baby stuff?"

So for kids thirteen and older, use a discipline list (*see Appendix C for a Sample Discipline List*)—it is the same exact concept, but on a list instead of a box. Remember, make the disciplines age-appropriate. If you have several teenagers, they can all use the same list: wash mom's car, wash dad's car, vacuum the inside of mom's car, wash five windows inside and out, and so on and so forth. These are disciplines that are over and above their normal chores. Mom, think of all that spring cleaning that you hate doing, put those things on the list—things that take between five and fifteen minutes.

When they break a rule, and the discipline list is the discipline for that rule instead of a related discipline, they go to that list, read the next discipline, and go do it. When they get to the bottom of the list, they start over. Obviously, if the discipline is to go out and sweep the back patio and it is 9:00 at night, you have the option, "OK, I want it done tomorrow before 3:00" and/or, "No, go to the next one on the list that you can do right now in the house." But you should not say, "Go do the worst one on the list that you hate."

Chores for Teens

Chores are a powerful training tool and teach your children some great work ethics as well, instilling character, personal responsibility, and self-control. *See Appendix D for a Sample Chore List.*

Five important ingredients for success in using chores correctly:

1. Make them fair. Let me give you an example. You have an eleven-year-old girl who washes dishes five nights a week, and you have a ten-year-old boy that only has to mow a 5' by 5' piece of grass once a week. Is that fair? No, it is not. A ten-year-old boy can learn how to do dishes, cook, and learn to fend for himself in the kitchen.

2. Make them age-appropriate. Be sensitive about what they can handle. Example: asking an eight-year old to wash your car may be beyond their ability.

3. Write them out. Just like the rules, chores need to be written down.

4. Determine in writing when those chores must be completed, day and time. For example, if the trash needs to be out Wednesday night because at 6:00 am on Thursday the trash truck comes, you do not want to be in this type of situation: your son comes home from school, "Hey, today's Wednesday, you've got to take the trash out."

"OK."

"Hey, it's dinner time; did you take the trash out?"

"No, I will after dinner."

"You'd better do it right after dinner." But after dinner, he sits down in front of the TV, and an hour later you say, "Turn that TV off, go take the trash out."

"Wait until after this show, Mom."

"You'd better do it now!" Then at bedtime, "Did you take the trash out! Now you're going to have to get up early tomorrow morning and do it." But the next morning, guess what you are doing at 5:45?

So, "the trash must be out by 6:00 pm on Wednesday." Which means that at 6:01, if that trash is not out, no matter what he is doing, short of something very personal in the bathroom, he is taking that trash out *right then*. And on top of that, because he waited until 6:01, he also does a discipline. Use the discipline box or the list for your discipline.

5. Train, do not nag. Stop the arguing, nagging and threatening—follow through.

What About Allowance?

I am a firm believer that allowance should not be tied to the actual work they do. Otherwise, you will find yourself in the situation that, when Mom comes home asks for help bringing in the groceries, your kids will respond, "How much money do I get?"

So I encourage you, especially when your children are younger, if you plan on giving them an allowance, to think about how many hours of chores you give them in a week's period, and come up with a dollar amount that you agree to as a couple. Then you simply say, "OK, I'm going to give you $5 a week because I love you and for helping. It's your spending money."

Cash burned a hole in Nick's pocket. He always wanted money; he always had something he wanted to buy. So I would tie dollar amounts to certain projects as a way for him to earn money over and above those normal chores.

When I have a special project I need help with, I warn my kids, "Hey, next Saturday, guys, I'll need your help in the morning. We're going to spend from 9:00 to 10:30 on this project." Sometimes I pay them for that, but I believe it is good to teach children to participate in keeping up the house without expecting to be paid.

And a servant of the Lord must not quarrel but be gentle to all, able to teach, patient, in humility correcting those who are in opposition, if God perhaps will grant them repentance, so that they may know the truth, and that they may come to their senses and escape the snare of the devil, having been taken captive by him to do his will.

—2 Timothy 2:24-26

God tells us to train up our children with a gentle reproof (Eph. 6:4). Clear, defined boundaries, clear defined disciplines, and consistency are so important.

In the next chapter we will discuss how to take all of this information you have acquired and begin to implement it in your home, no matter where you are starting from.

CHAPTER FIFTEEN

Starting Over

Every year I speak to many parents around the US and abroad, and their most common response to this material is, "Why haven't I ever heard these things before? I've been a Christian for twenty years. Why haven't I ever understood these scripture verses in application to the relationship I have with my children?"

Some of you may even have older children who have already left the home. After reading this book, you may be thinking, "Oh, no wonder they're so angry with me. No wonder our relationship is so bad. I can see how my parenting style affected them."

I am well aware that a large percentage of you need to say to your children, "We need to start over."

The question now is: how can you effectively implement the strategies and tools from the preceding chapters, especially if your kids are teenagers or adult children living in your home?

First, please stop and remember: God waited until now to expose you to this material. He does not operate in the same time frame we do. So the question is: why did God wait until now? Not so that you would feel defeated and condemned, but so that at the right time, according to His foreknowledge, you would be ready and able to change your relationship with your children.

So what can you do about a strained relationship? Everything! You can literally start over. Even if your children are out of your house, there are some important steps you can take.

Obviously you are not going to bring your kids back home and start over with your discipline, if they have moved out or away. But when it comes to relationships, every day is a new day to start over.

You should be the one to reach out first. When I first came to Christ, one of the most difficult things God asked me to do was to go back and forgive my father. It was hard, believe me, but it was worth it.

Simple Steps

Step One: Confess Your Own Sins to the Lord.

The first step in restoring a right relationship with your children is to confess your own sins to the Lord:

"He who covers his sins will not prosper, but whoever confesses and forsakes them will have mercy" (Prov. 28:13).

"If we confess our sins, He is faithful and just to forgive us our sins and to cleanse us from all unrighteousness" (1 John 1:9).

As you have read this material, God has likely been bringing to your mind behaviors you have made part of your discipline routine, which you now know are sin. Remember, God is not angry with you; He is simply bringing the truth to light at this point so that you can change.

What you must do is say, "I see that it was sin, God. Please forgive me." Every sinful word or activity God has revealed to you (even the things you did not do that you should have done), confess them to the Lord. Don't be vague — try and be very specific with the Lord. Remember, the things we did not do, like not leading properly, not discipling our children, or not being consistent with our discipline, all need to be confessed also.

"Father, I know I failed, I'm sorry."

Step Two: Ask for Forgiveness

Secondly, once you have confessed and sought forgiveness from the Lord, you need to ask for forgiveness from the other person in the relationship: the one affected by your words, deed, or lack of deeds.

"Therefore if you bring your gift to the altar, and there remember that your brother has something against you, leave your gift there before the altar, and go your way. First be reconciled to your brother, and then come and offer your gift" (Matt. 5:23-24).

Does it matter if you have an eighteen-month old who does not even understand your language yet? No. If you have failed him, screaming and yelling in response to his childishness rather than patiently training him, you need to go to him and say, "I'm sorry, Son, what Daddy (or what Mommy) did was wrong."

Go to that person you have offended, be very specific about the things you did wrong, and ask him or her to forgive you. "Please forgive me for yelling. Please forgive me for saying those harsh words. Please forgive me for not being unified and/or consistent." Be specific.

"Be angry, and do not sin": do not let the sun go down on your wrath" (Eph. 4:26).

So often we allow our sinful behavior, and the bitterness and harshness that accompany it, to go on and on, and then we just go to bed as if it never happened. God wants us to stop that sinful routine. We need to be in a place where we are humble enough to ask for forgiveness.

Every time you yelled and screamed at your kids, it was like slicing their hearts with a knife. If you do not ask for forgiveness, and apply the salve of healing (which is asking for forgiveness), infection will set in, then resentment, and then revenge. Many of you reading this book may have kids who are already angry and bitter and hurt because you have sliced them over and over and over again and never applied the salve of forgiveness.

When you ask for forgiveness, you are wiping the antidote God has given you on their hearts and beginning the healing process. This is so very important. If we do not practice this daily towards our children, as we are growing and being transformed ourselves, then we can become the greatest tool of our enemy to harden our children's heart, so the seeds of discipleship or discipline will not penetrate their hard hearts and take root.

Remember, there is absolutely no justification for our sinful behavior. We must take full responsibility.

Step Three: Forgive

Third, you need to learn to forgive others—especially your children. Even now, you may be thinking, "Well, what about when my kids hurt me? I'm still so angry at my daughter for taking my car on a joy ride that cost me eight hundred dollars to fix. What do I do with that?"

> *Therefore, as the elect of God, holy and beloved, put on tender mercies, kindness, humility, meekness, longsuffering; bearing with one another, and forgiving one another, if anyone has a complaint against another; even as Christ forgave you, so you also must do.*
> —Colossians 3:12-13

You must remember that you are Christ's minister to His children, and, as such, you must have the mindset of continuous forgiveness.

"*And be kind to one another, tenderhearted, forgiving one another, even as God in Christ forgave you*" (Eph. 4:32).

You need to forgive your children constantly. Let whatever it is go, today. Believe me, I realize some of the mistakes our kids make can be big ones, and they can be costly. But you have to let it go. It is a choice, an act of obedience to God. Do not wait until you feel like it.

Four Points of Forgiveness

Point One:

Once you forgive others, including your children, you cannot keep a record of the wrongs you suffered.

Love *". . . keeps no record of wrong"* (1 Cor. 13:5). This means you cannot continuously bring up your children's failures. Unfortunately, many parents do this, constantly bringing up things that happened in the past to use against them today. That is not true forgiveness.

If you have that bad habit, it is important that you get rid of it. And now that you have new tools and strategies, you are going to deal with the discipline at the moment, not drag it out for days or weeks.

Point Two:

Do not gossip to others about your children's failures or sins. Obviously it is acceptable to discuss discipline issues between husband and wife, but not in front of your kids or to a friend.

When I come home and my son or daughter has misbehaved, my wife does not come up and just blurt out, "You know what he did today . . . blah blah blah." That is not appropriate.

One day, my wife and my daughter had a bad day homeschooling together. I came home that night, and I could tell it had been a rough day. So my wife and I went to the movies that night, and my wife explained all the details of what had taken place, and how she had handled the problems.

At bedtime that night, I prayed with Katie, and one of the things she prayed was: "I pray that Mommy and I have a good day tomorrow."

I kissed her when she was finished, and said, "Yeah, I heard you had a rough day."

She was surprised, "You know?"

I said, "Of course I know."

I could see her trying to read my expression, thinking, "Isn't he mad?"

I merely said, "I bet you're going to have a better day tomorrow. I love you, Honey," gave her a kiss, and walked out. The situation was dealt with, and Katie never had to bear the embarrassment of hearing her mom lay out all her shortcomings.

Point Three:
You cannot dwell on the offenses of others.

Finally, brethren, whatever things are true, whatever things are noble, whatever things are just, whatever things are pure, whatever things are lovely, whatever things are of good report, if there is any virtue and if there is anything praiseworthy—meditate on these things.
—Philippians 4:8

Let it go. Do not allow past mistakes to dictate your current attitude. True forgiveness entails assuming and hoping the best of your children, not eagerly waiting for the next mistake to occur.

"If it is possible, as much as depends on you, live peaceably with all men" (Rom. 12:18).

You must understand that your children may have some deep-seated bitterness and anger toward you. You may have to face a very angry teenager, and despite your best intentions, you must realize that when you ask for forgiveness, she may not forgive you: "Yeah, I've heard 'sorry' before, but you've been screaming and yelling for as long as I can remember."

You need to reach out to your children, but do not expect them to say, "OK, thanks," and embrace you. They are going to watch you; they are going to test you. That is a normal thing.

Point Four:
Forgiveness is to be granted without limitation.

> *Then Peter came to Him and said, "Lord, how often shall my brother sin against me, and I forgive him? Up to seven times?"*
> *Jesus said to him, "I do not say to you, up to seven times, but up to seventy times seven."*
> —Matthew 18:21-22

As ministers, when can we stop forgiving our children? Never!

We must have a continuous mind set that we will forgive them, no matter what they do, even when they do things deliberately to hurt us. Our job is to train them. Yes, it is hard. Standing on that inner strength: God's Word and the power of the Holy Spirit are the only way we can do this.

Parenting is difficult; it is not for cowards.

Reconciliation—Setting up the Family Meeting

Now it is time to sit down with your kids and explain to them the things you have learned. In a two-parent family, the husband and wife should meet first and pray over and agree upon the important points. Prayerfully write out your rules, discipline, appropriate punishments, and chores for each of your children.

You need to remember you are not doing this because you are frustrated with your children's behavior, because you are sick of the chaos, or because of the attitudes of your kids. You are doing this because God wants you to. He has revealed His truth to you, so you are making changes in response.

Please note: if one of your children has a serious relationship problem with either of the parents, the parents should meet individually with that child before the family meeting takes place. Otherwise, if you sit down with the whole group first, and begin explaining what you are going to do, that particular child will have the attitude of, "Yeah, right," which may dampen the response of the other children.

Open this one-on-one meeting with prayer, then humbly acknowledge the past problem, and seek reconciliation with that child by asking for their forgiveness for the mistakes that you have made. Be specific. Dad you start. Mom, you're next. Once you have said your piece, it is important that you give your child an opportunity to respond. However, do not be upset if they remain silent.

I have had many reconciliation meetings in my office; I love seeing the tears and unity that God brings in those meetings, how the Holy Spirit blesses them. But it does not always go down that way. Many times the child does not respond right away. And that is OK.

Make sure you have your rules, discipline, appropriate punishments, and chore lists written out before you set up a family meeting. Provide a copy of each list to each of your children, with the exception of kids that cannot yet read. Simply show your younger kids the lists and then hold onto them. Later, you can post them in their rooms; I will return to that idea later in the chapter.

Again, begin the meeting with prayer, asking God for His help and guidance in your home. Fathers, I exhort you to be the one to lead the prayer, even if you have never prayed in front of your kids before. Yes, you will probably freak them out, but do it anyhow. Prove to them that you are asking for God's help in this thing.

Apologize, if necessary, to your children as a group. Ask them to forgive you for your mistakes, your sins, and your lack of understanding of proper parenting thus far.

Even if you have already said these things to one of the children individually, it is important that your other children see what went on between you and this child. Asking forgiveness again, collectively, shows humility. That one child knows the other kids saw you constantly yell and scream at him; your acknowledgement of this in front of all the kids emphasizes your sincerity.

It may sound something like this: "Some things have been brought to Mom's and my attention, things that we've been doing wrong as parents. And we already sat down with Johnny and asked for him to forgive us for what we've been saying and doing to him. But we want to say this to all of you kids, for the yelling and the screaming, the inconsistency, we're sorry."

Again, give your children an opportunity to voice their feelings, but do not require them to. I strongly suggest, Dads, you start by asking for forgiveness, and Moms, be willing and ready to ask for forgiveness also, for any specific sins the Lord has revealed to you. Dads, you need to be leading this discussion.

Finally, explain the rules and discipline, punishment and chores for each one of your children. Make sure that you communicate to them that these changes are not taking place because they have been bad or have done something wrong, and you are now forcing marshal law upon them. Instead, be sure to explain what discipline is all about:

First, explain that *discipline is biblical,* and that God is holding you accountable for the way you train up your children.

Second, explain the *difference between discipline and punishment* and the reasons behind them (see Tool Numbers Two and Three in chapter Eleven for clarity).

Third, give them the definition of a *mature adult,* and explain that your God-given responsibility is to lovingly train them to become those mature adults (see sections entitled Bring Them Up; Hitting the Bull's-Eye; and Definition of a Mature Adult in chapter Ten).

Fourth, persuade them that the *family is a team,* and everyone needs to work together so that the home will be a refuge and a place of peace for all family members.

Fifth, explain the need and your desire for *weekly family devotions,* and let them know the day and time that the weekly devotions will take place.

In terms of your devotions, I recommend you have one for the smaller kids and one for the older kids, if possible. In some homes, mothers work with the younger children while fathers do devotions with the older ones, which is just fine. But be careful, fathers. If you are a believer, do not use this as an excuse to pass the whole thing off onto Mom. You are the priest of your household. You must take that responsibility very seriously. It is also one of your wife's companionship needs that she needs from you, for you to be the spiritual leader.

Even though my wife was doing the Bible studies for my daughter in the morning, I took responsibility, I was involved. I went over the Bible study with her almost every single day at our prayer time in the evening. Now I do a weekly Bible study along with discussing her own daily devotional time with her.

A Short Transition Period

Be forewarned that if you have had very little structure in your home prior to this, your children will not jump for joy. Allow some grace on enforcing your discipline for the first week or so. What that means is, if you have been spending time arguing and debating, letting them slide on issues like chores for the last four years, you need to clearly lay out the new plan: "I'm going to remind you once for the next five days, but after that, there will be no more reminding."

If you have allowed this arguing to go on for a long time, now that you have defined "respect" and implemented appropriate discipline, if the conversations become heated, you simply say, "Hold it, Honey. I know this is something we used to do, but remember this is an area of disrespect. So I'm warning you right now, pull it together." Then, if they continue, you need to follow through and give them the predetermined discipline.

So do allow that grace period, but a week later, remind them, "OK, grace period is over. Now we're all back on track."

Be Sensitive

Once the new system is up and running for a while, you may discover that some of your rules and disciplines are unfair or too harsh. You do need to be sensitive to God's guidance as you evaluate how the system is working.

Parents contact me quite often, trying to decide what is appropriate and what is not. One father of a seventeen-year old wondered if a 9:00 pm bedtime was inappropriate, since his son was having a problem with it. I told him, "Yeah, I do think 9:00 pm is pretty early for a seventeen-year old."

I asked the boy, "How late do you want to be up?"

He replied, "At least until 10:00 pm."

"Dad, what do you think?"

"I guess that's OK."

"Good, are you OK to change your rule."

If the kids are strenuously objecting, and you think the rule may be too harsh, seek the Lord and get some counsel. Fathers, be ready to listen and consider your wife's input; it will be important here. If you decide the rule is too harsh, change it. Remember, your family is a team.

Post the rules and discipline list in an essential area of your home, like the kitchen. No, I do not encourage putting it in plain sight on the refrigerator, especially if you have older kids. Their friends come over and cannot resist the refrigerator, then you have, "What's this?" Small kids do not care where you post it, but when they get older, they are more sensitive about such things.

Instead, put it inside a kitchen cabinet, a drawer, a closet or something, and give the kids their own copies as well. Your teenager is probably not going to want to post it in his room. Do not force him to, simply give him a copy. Of course he will probably lose it or throw it away. That's why you post your own copy.

Follow-up Family Meetings

A follow-up family meeting should be held every two months for the next six months. It is important that you sit down with the kids and say, "OK, how are we doing?" You might have to shore some things up in some cases that have begun to slide back into old habits. Come together as a family and discuss these things. However, do not make this a time of negotiation. You are still in charge.

It is also vitally important for husband and wife to communicate regularly with each other about how things are progressing, as when my wife told me about her rough home schooling day with Katie and how she had resolved it. It is so important to be involved, to engage. However, moms, if you stay home, when Dad comes home from work, do not blast him the minute he walks in the door with all the bad things that happened that day. The house is supposed to be a refuge. Wait for the right time to discuss these things with him.

Examine Yourself Often

Finally, you need to evaluate your progress periodically. Of course, the first thing you look at should be: is Jesus still my cornerstone? Because, as you know, your spiritual foundation (which is your daily devotional time) is the most important aspect of fulfilling your job as a minister. Then begin to look at your relationship with your children:

Are you responding to them in love, or in anger?

Are you communicating your love with time and proper affection?

Are you discipling as well as disciplining?

Is your system of discipline based on God's management style? (See chapter Eight.)

It is so important that you check up on yourself, because if any one of these things gets out of order, the whole thing can start unraveling.

Remember, God blesses obedience, and so if you obediently apply these principles that you have learned, you are going to see God intercede, and you will begin to understand when He speaks to you specifically about how your home should work and what rules you should have.

God so desires you to have success in training up your children in the way they should go! It is my deepest hope and desire that the principles and tools you have learned in this book will assist you in achieving that goal. Remember: God doesn't do by miracle what He's called you to do by obedience.

Please visit our website, www.parentingministry.org, for additional information and material, or to contact us. There is a detailed video series with a workbook available that can help you in implementing these principles, along with a leaders' guide to help you teach others.

Now, go and minister to the gifts God has given to you: your children!

APPENDIX

Appendix A

SAMPLE FAMILY RULES AND DISCIPLINES

Child's Name _____

Examples for 18 months to 5 years-old

Rule 1:   **Respect one another at all times – parents and siblings.**

Discipline   Time out (5 to 10 minutes – use timer)

Rule 2:   **No physical fighting or verbal arguing.**

Discipline   Time out and/or separate for 15 minutes – use the timer. The first one who talks to the other gets another discipline. Don't try to be the judge and jury every time.

Rule 3:   **Help clean up your own messes, toys, etc.**

Discipline   Time out and (if a toy) toy gets put away for two days.

Appendix B

SAMPLE FAMILY RULES AND DISCIPLINES

Child's Name _____

Examples for ages 6 and older

Rule 1: **Respect one another at all times. Respect both parents always.**

Discipline   Draw one item from the discipline box or list.

Rule 2: **No physical fighting or verbal arguing.**

Discipline   Draw one item from discipline box, if physical add ½ day room restriction.

Rule 3: **Be ready for school by 7:15 a.m.**

Discipline   Be awakened at 5:00 a.m. the following morning or go to bed ½ hour early.

Rule 4: **Clean up your own messes expediently.**

Discipline   Draw one item from the discipline box or list and clean up mess.

Rule 5: **Return home by the specified time from an approved outing.**

Discipline   Home restriction for two days.

Rule 6: **Telephone privileges until 9:00 p.m. (with approval).**

Discipline   No telephone privileges for two days.

Appendix C

SAMPLE DISCIPLINE LIST

Age 13 and above

1. Vacuum a particular room									
2. Clean all mirrors in bath									
3. Clean sink and bathtub in bathroom									
4. Clean toilet									
5. Clean behind couch, silk flower in basket, & TV									
6. Clean up backyard – dog									
7. Mow the backyard									

8. Pull weeds in front yard for 10'x20' area or 15 min.									
9. Water back yard – 20 minutes									
10. Water front yard – 15 minutes									
11. Wash four windows inside and out									
12. Wash car									
13. Vacuum inside of car									
14. Sweep garage									
15. Clean out refrigerator									

Appendix D

SAMPLE CHORE LIST

Child's Name

_____

Chore: **Feed the dog**
_____

Day: Everyday   Time by: 5 p.m.

Discipline   Discipline Box or List
_____

Chore: **Take the trash out**
_____

Day: Wednesdays   Time by: 6 p.m.

Discipline   Discipline Box or List
_____

Chore: **Clean the bathroom**
_____

Day: Saturdays   Time by: 8 p.m.

Discipline   Discipline Box or List
_____

Chore: **Mow the grass**

Day: Saturdays   Time by: 5 p.m.

Discipline   Discipline Box or List

Chore: **Vacuum living room & dust**

Day: Saturdays   Time by: 8 p.m.

Discipline   Discipline Box or List

Appendix E

Parent's Questionnaire for Youth Turning Age 18

(Revealing the parents' reality vs. the child's possible delusion)

The following questions are designed for discussion with your child just prior to his or her 18th birthday. They are most effective when discussed in a relaxed setting, for the purpose of stimulating your child to think, and to encourage a more adult relationship with your child as they are entering adulthood. It will also reveal what they believe is going to change in their relationship with you.

Give one copy to your child to fill out & one copy for you to fill out. Set a date and time when you will sit down with your child to discuss their answers and share your answers (true reality) with them.

1. At 18 what do mom and I owe you besides our love?

   _____
   _____
   _____

2. Do you believe that the reason we help you the way we do is because we love you?

   ☐ Yes ☐ No

3. Should we be doing more for you than we are currently doing?
    ☐ Yes ☐ No

    If *yes*, what should we be doing?

4. Do we have the right to require anything of you in return for you continuing to live in our home?
    ☐ Yes   ☐ No Explain.

    _____
    _____
    _____

5. If you do not agree with something we ask or require of you what should you do?

    _____
    _____
    _____

6. If you ignore our request and do something that we have made clear not to do, what do you think we should do? What should you do?

    _____
    _____
    _____